POLITICAL ECONOMY NOW!

The struggle for alternative economics
at the University of Sydney

Compiled by
Gavan Butler, Evan Jones and Frank Stilwell

Published 2009 by Darlington Press
Darlington Press is an imprint of SYDNEY UNIVERSITY PRESS
Fisher Library, University of Sydney
www.sup.usyd.edu.au

© Gavan Butler, Evan Jones and Frank Stilwell 2009
© Darlington Press 2009

Compiled by Gavan Butler, Evan Jones and Frank Stilwell for the Australian Political Economy Movement. Additional research assistance by Kirrily Jordan and Nadia Yetton-Lim; and editorial assistance by Sandra Goldbloom Zurbo.

Reproduction and Communication for other purposes

Except as permitted under the Act, no part of this edition may be reproduced, stored in a retrieval system, or communicated in any form or by any means without prior written permission. All requests for reproduction or communication should be made to Darlington Press at the address below:

Fisher Library F03, University of Sydney, NSW Australia 2006
Email: info@sup.usyd.edu.au

National Library of Australia Cataloguing-in-Publication entry

Author:	Butler, Gavan.
Title:	Political economy now! : the struggle for alternative economics at the University of Sydney / Gavan Butler, Evan Jones, Frank Stilwell.
ISBN:	9781921364051 (pbk.)
Notes:	Bibliography.
Subjects:	University of Sydney. Faculty of Arts. Dept. of Political Economy.
	Economics--Study and teaching (Higher)--New South Wales--Sydney.
	Schools of economics--Study and teaching (Higher)--New South Wales--Sydney.
	Economics--Political aspects.
Other Authors/Contributors:	
	Jones, Evan, 1944-
	Stilwell, Frank J. B.
Dewey Number:	330.1099441

Cover design by Miguel Yamin, the University Publishing Service

Since the founding of the University the conviction we then had has been growing upon us, that no department of study is more imperatively required to be provided for than the whole science of Political Economy. The public is well aware that this branch of knowledge has been entirely overlooked in the arrangements of that Institution ... By Political Economy we mean something more extensive than what is usually understood by the phrase. The name is commonly applied to commercial and financial science exclusively. In our opinion it should include the whole range of public and general social relations, duties, and interests as objects of practical concern ... The science exists, and imperatively calls, side by side with the philosophy of which it is to be the application, for the endowment of a professorship.

The Empire, Monday 2 January 1854, excerpt from the editorial. *The Empire* was a newspaper published in Sydney between 1850–75, and edited between 1850–58 by Henry Parkes.

*This book is dedicated to all students of political economy
—past, present and future*

Contents

Contents v
Introduction vii

1. Emerging conflict 1
2. Getting started 21
3. Resolve or resign! 40
4. More struggles 55
5. A long march 76
6. A significant shift 90
7. What's wrong with economics? 104
8. Pedagogy and power 118
9. Intellectual suppression 134
10. Market forces 148
11. Dissent and legitimacy 159
12. Whither political economy? 181

Chronology of principal events 193
Index 207

Introduction

This is the story of one of the most substantial and enduring conflicts in the history of Australian universities. The conflict was centred on the Faculty of Economics at the University of Sydney. It was an acrimonious struggle between those committed to the teaching of mainstream economics and the proponents of alternative courses in political economy—PE. It began in the 1960s and continued for decades until a Department of Political Economy was established in the Faculty of Arts in 2008. The book's title—*Political Economy Now!*—echoes a chant commonly heard at the many student demonstrations during the first two decades of the struggle:

>What do we want?
>Political economy!
>When do we want it?
>Now!

Why all the fuss over the teaching of economics? Why were the disagreements so deep and protracted? What has been at stake? Why did dissident staff and students commit so much time and energy to establishing and developing alternative courses and administrative arrangements?

The political economy dispute can be regarded as a classic, albeit extreme, example of academic conflict: it involved substantial differences of opinion about the nature of the curriculum, the style of teaching, and the structures of power and decision making within the university. On one side, orthodoxy was defended and professorial authority was asserted. On the other, dissident students and academic staff, pressing their claims for a different type of education, organised protests that included numerous public meetings, petitions, leaflets and posters, noisy demonstrations, strikes and sit-ins. There were confrontations with university security and police. One student was arrested, nine were suspended and another four subjected to disciplinary procedures by the University. Four tutors had their employment prematurely terminated. Articles about the dispute frequently appeared in the mainstream media as well as in the student press. Numerous committees were established by governing bodies within the University that sought resolution of the ongoing conflict. To its credit, the University permitted both sides to coexist, but it was not a peaceful coexistence. The University's official commitment to tolerance of different academic viewpoints seemed at odds with its evident difficulty in comfortably accommodating the contestants.

Although locally focused at the University of Sydney and peaking in intensity during the 1970s and 1980s, the dispute also has wider and continuing implications for how we understand the economic system and the role of economic policy. To a degree the conflict between mainstream economists and political economists can be regarded as reflecting a broader tension in Australian society, a tension about the pros and cons of what came to be known in the 1980s and 1990s as 'economic rationalism'. Influential in public policy, this doctrine had its roots in mainstream economic theory, and in neoclassical economics in particular. The mainstream includes neoliberals, who regard government intervention to counter adverse market outcomes as usually doing more harm than good, and liberal interventionists who are more accepting of a need for selective adjustment policies. Political economists, though quite diverse in their views about how the economy should be analysed and reconstructed, generally take a more critical perspective on market outcomes, from which follows a perception of an organic relation between politics and the economy.

Their politics tends towards a less benign view of capitalism and its capacity to deliver economic outcomes that are efficient, equitable and sustainable.

In the Faculty of Economics at the University of Sydney at the end of the 1960s, there were essentially three disciplines—economics, accounting, and government and public administration—which together dominated the structure of the Bachelor of Economics degree. Economic history and economic statistics had been established as small offshoots from economics, as would industrial relations later. The teaching of economics itself, as in universities in all Anglophone countries, was being wrenched into a pattern that involved a core of courses in theory (microeconomics and macroeconomics), followed by a range of electives in applied fields that were available after students had undertaken the core courses. An elective or two on the history of economic thought was available as an acknowledgement that the subject had been marked by different perspectives, even if none other than the neoclassical perspective had turned out to be worth understanding. Economics was to be concerned with market behaviour, whereas the study of power and politics was considered best left to a different department (such as Government and Public Administration in the case of the University of Sydney).

The principal forces for the assertion of this orthodoxy at the University of Sydney were Colin Simkin and Warren Hogan, two professors appointed to the Department of Economics in the late 1960s. Simkin and Hogan had the support of Bruce Williams, who had been a professor of economics in the UK before being appointed as Vice-Chancellor of the University of Sydney in 1967. There was early resistance to Simkin and Hogan's course reforms, both by tutors and by other more senior academics who were resentful of the lack of consultation by the new professors and of the curriculum changes themselves. These academics included Ted Wheelwright, who was well known as a left-wing economist, and Geelum Simpson-Lee, who would later became dean of the faculty, as well as Maurice Haddad, Louis Haddad, Margaret Power and Hugh Pritchard. They were joined by Debesh Bhattycharya, Gavan Butler, Frank Stilwell and Evan Jones, four young lecturers appointed from abroad who also had qualms about the narrowness of mainstream economics. These dissidents joined a growing number of concerned students in becoming advocates of political economy courses as an alternative to the mainstream economics favoured by Professors Hogan and Simkin.

So what is political economy? The term has strong historical roots. It was widely used during the eighteenth and nineteenth centuries. Classical political economy encompassed the works of Adam Smith, David Ricardo, Thomas Malthus and the later proponents of economic liberalism in the first half of the nineteenth century, such as James and John Stuart Mill. Karl Marx developed a critique of classical political economy and then formulated his own theory of political economy.[1] The term 'economics' came to replace 'political economy' in the wake of the marginalist revolution that ushered in neoclassical theory towards the end of the nineteenth century. That latter theoretical approach, dominant ever since, is based on individualism, a subjective theory of value and the notion that adjustments in individuals' choices occur in small increments that can be analysed by means of the calculus.

Neoclassical economics is preoccupied with exchange and the decision rules that individual economic agents should employ, whereas the various non-neoclassical approaches share a concern for

---

[1] For a discussion of classical and Marxian political economy, see, for example, Ian Bradley & Michael Howard (eds), *Classical and Marxian political economy: essays in honour of Ronald L. Meek*, Macmillan, London and Basingstoke, 1982.

explaining production as a social phenomenon. Non-neoclassical approaches seek to explain how production is organised, how it is controlled so that there is a surplus of production in any given period over a society's needs for its reproduction, and how this surplus is used.[2] They embrace, *inter alia*, Marxian and neo-Marxist economics, ideas drawn from the tradition of institutional economists, an approach that is founded in the work of David Ricardo[3] and the work of the many writers who recognise the self-conscious pursuit and exercise of power by human agents (by, for example, the patriarchs of Western societies, private corporations and some holders of public office). University teaching of economics since the 1960s has generally privileged the place of neoclassical economics and marginalised these other approaches. At the University of Sydney the proponents of political economy contested the structures supporting this bias.

The use of the term 'political economy' at the University of Sydney reflected, first, a repudiation of the view that economics is defined principally in terms of the neoclassical tradition in economic thought, and, second, the belief that twentieth-century developments of classical, Marxian and institutional political economy provide better ways of understanding the contemporary world than does neoclassical theory. A strong emphasis is placed on analysing the distribution of income and wealth and the role of the state in the economy. Feminist

---

[2] See Mauro Baranzini and Roberto Scazzieri, 'Knowledge in economics: a framework,' in Baranzini and Scazzieri (eds), *Foundations of economics: structures of inquiry and economic theory*, Blackwell, Oxford and New York, 1986; and Robert L. Heilbroner, *The nature and logic of capitalism*, W.W. Norton, New York and London, 1985.

[3] Ricardo's influence on modern political economy is significantly due to the twentieth-century economist, Pierro Sraffa; see Bradley & Howard, *op. cit.*, especially papers by the editors and by Ian Steedman.

and environmental concerns have also been reflected in the development of modern political economy.

The struggle between the mainstream economists and the political economists was never just a matter of a contest of ideas within economics as a discipline. It was also a struggle about students' and academics' rights. It raised fundamental issues about the role of educational institutions, including questions about what should be taught and who should make such decisions. The need in teaching to demonstrate the usefulness of a paradigm or theories, rather than to assert authority, was a recurrent theme. So, too, was the need to draw students into thinking about economics from the starting point of their own perceptions as young adults living in the society at large. The political economists argued that students should participate in the design of their education—to help draw up curricula, to question what is laid down by the writers of textbooks, and to actively participate in the assessment of their progress in learning. The embrace of these progressive and participatory educational principles was met with unremitting hostility by the professors of economics. Their authoritarian attitude—for that is what it was—also extended to the matter of how much say academic staff in general could have in designing curricula, methods of teaching and assessment methods. The moves towards democratisation of the governance of the University that gained momentum in the 1970s directly challenged their professorial authority.

The concern with pedagogy and authority in academic learning was not peculiar to economics at the University of Sydney. It arose in other disciplines,[4] and in economics it had arisen earlier outside

---

[4] Antecedents in this struggle included the *Free University* established in Sydney during the late 1960s, by, among others, R.W. Connell and Terry Irving of the Department of Government and Public Administration (see the one issue of *Free U* published c. 1969).

Australia. In the USA, for example, there had been a dispute in economics at Harvard University that led to the removal of a group of young radical economists, including Sam Bowles and Herb Gintis,[5] who were subsequently employed at the University of Massachusetts, Amherst, which then became a centre of political economic research and teaching. Bowles and Gintis came to the first national political economy conference held in Australia in 1976, a conference that gave a great boost to the confidence of political economists in Sydney and across the nation. There had also been a campaign for the reform of teaching on various US campuses, such as the University of California at Berkeley.[6] Challenges to conventional courses were linked to broader concerns about education, equity and freedom. It was common during the political economy dispute at the University of Sydney for students and younger staff to make reference to the works of Paulo Freire and Ivan Illich, respectively *Pedagogy of the oppressed* and *Deschooling society*.[7]

The struggle for political economy took a large part of many lives. It impaired the research productivity of several of the academics

---

[5] An early, widely influential work was Samuel Bowles and Herbert Gintis, *Schooling in capitalist America: educational reform and the contradictions of economic life*, Routledge and Kegan Paul, London, 1976.

[6] At Berkeley, a Board of Educational Development functioned provocatively during the years 1967 to 1970. For an indication of its concerns, see *Guide to Board of Educational Development reports*, University Archives, Bancroft Library, University of California, Berkeley.

[7] For example, Paulo Freire, *Pedagogy of the oppressed*, Penguin, Harmondsworth, 1972, and Ivan Illich, *Deschooling society*, Marion Boyars, London, 2000 (1st edn c. 1970). Note was also taken of Herbert Gintis, 'Towards a political economy of education: a radical critique of Ivan Illich's *Deschooling society*,' in Alan Gartner, Colin Greer and Frank Riessman (eds), *After deschooling, what?*, Perennial, London, 1973.

involved and damaged the prospects of a few of the more vigorously protesting students. Some commentators said it damaged the reputation of the University and the Faculty of Economics (as it then was), and undoubtedly it did so in the eyes of particular conservative elements in society, people who claimed that the struggle impaired the employability of students ('irresponsible student radicals') and that the curriculum that the political economists sought to establish would not adequately prepare students for jobs that economics graduates could normally expect. Journalists Padraic P. McGuinness and David Clark were particularly strident in their accusation that the proponents of PE sacrificed students' prospects to an exercise in 'left-wing adventurism'.[8]

The struggle also enriched many lives. Over the years the numerous student participants experienced an active engagement in questioning established orthodoxies, to the benefit of their own learning and, more generally, their personal development. Moreover, for every corporate job that might have become less accessible—and perhaps less attractive—to them, many more employment opportunities opened up in organisations where a sound generalist education was valued. Economic journalism and the media became distinctive focal points, as did jobs in public service, trade union research, financial institutions and NGOs. The restoration of an economics pathway that actually prepared graduates for dealing with practical concerns beyond the mathematical modelling favoured by mainstream economists was one of the most important achievements of the struggle for political economy. There were others, as the story that follows will establish.

---

[8] See, for example, P.P. McGuiness, *National Times*, 24 March 1975, and *Australian Financial Review*, 20 July 1976 and 31 January 1989; and D. Clark, *Australian Financial Review*, 9 February 1987 and 15 February 1988, and *Australian Student News*, April 1988.

There were some particularly dramatic and polarising episodes during the heady and exhausting protests, demonstrations and arguments that spread over almost all of the two decades of the 1970s and 1980s at the University of Sydney. In 1974, for example, political economy student activists held a 'day of outrage' that drew attention to the lack of any resolution of the concerns that had led them to organise a 'day of protest' in the previous year. In 1975, students occupied the Vice-Chancellor's office (and consumed the contents of his cocktail cabinet). In 1976 there was a strike by about 4000 students and 100 university staff that lasted eleven days. In 1983, a later cohort of student activists occupied the University's clock tower to draw attention to their concerns. Shortly afterwards another group occupied the staff common room in the Faculty of Economics for ten days. Each episode drew condemnation from the University authorities. Concurrently, each could, in time, be seen as driving progress of sorts. The University authorities allowed political economy courses to be introduced and, bit by bit, these courses eventually developed into a full program that students could take as an alternative to the mainstream economics courses.

Different tensions developed in the 1990s and early 2000s as the commercial reorientation of tertiary education made the political economy program marginal to the principal concerns of the Faculty of Economics and Business (as it had by then become). In 2008, political economy was repositioned in a new School of Social and Political Sciences within the Faculty of Arts. This gave it the status, denied to it throughout the 1970s, 1980s and 1990s, of being a separate department. At the time of writing, over 1000 students were studying political economy at one level or another, adding to the approximately 12,000 students who had gone before them. Some of the past students have been among the best and brightest at the University of Sydney and many now hold prominent positions in government, commerce, educational institutions and throughout civil society. Recollections of some of them are included at the end of each chapter in this book.

The political economy dispute at the University of Sydney warrants documentation, not just because it is a striking example of institutional conflict, but also because of its broader social, political and economic significance. This volume provides that documentation, bringing together a general historical narrative, pictures, personal recollections and an interpretation of the causes and consequences of the dispute. As a counterpoint to official institutional histories,[9] it provides insight into how the conflict looked from the political economists' perspective. It is the story of the struggle for alternative economics.

Subsequent chapters explore the stages of conflict on the campus, the principal issues in dispute, the underlying problem of intellectual suppression, the influence of economic interests, the protestors' quest for legitimacy and the outcomes of the conflict. In this way the book shifts from considering the surface appearances of the dispute—the *minutiae* of faculty meetings, demonstrations, petitions and committees of inquiry—to considering its systemic nature, the

---

[9] See W.F. Connell, G. Sherington, B. Fletcher, C. Turvey & V. Bygott (eds), *Australia's first: a history of the University of Sydney, volume 2, 1940-1990*, University of Sydney, in association with Hale & Iremonger, Sydney, 1995, pp. 207-09 and 385-88. See also, P.D. Groenewegen, *Educating for business, public service and the social sciences: a history of the Faculty of Economics at the University of Sydney (1920-1999)* (Sydney University Press, forthcoming) and Bruce Williams, *Making and breaking universities: memoirs of an academic life in Australia and Britain, 1936-2004*, Macleay Press, Sydney, 2005. Because these principals of this story have spoken at length for themselves, through these writings, this absolves the authors from laboriously trying to set out their positions.

broader social and political context in which it occurred, and the key lessons to be drawn from it.

This book is written by participants in the dispute who have drawn upon their own experiences and recollections of the events. Some references to sources and related material are included in the footnotes but, for the most part, the sources from which each part of the story are drawn are not indicated in detail. For those who would wish to look more carefully at the relevant historical documents, the authors have lodged a comprehensive set in the Rare Books and Special Collections of the Fisher Library at the University of Sydney. It takes up the equivalent of about 3 metres of shelf space, including faculty documents, reports of official committees of inquiry, newspaper articles, personal correspondence and other evidence on which this more general narrative is based.

Figure 1. Political economy students posing during a protest outside the Quadrangle, 1975.

An early participant reflects: John Burgess

Postgraduate student and tutor in the Department of Economics in the 1970s; now Professor of Management at the University of Newcastle

It is easy with a suspect memory to reminisce about characters, events, feuds and drama. The PE struggle had it all and would make a good script for a television series that involved passion, treachery, comedy, tragedy, power, politics, lust and violence. Leaving aside the many personalities and the many specific events, there are still a few issues worth exploring. Looking back on the PE struggle four questions come to mind: Why did it happen? Why did it happen only at the University of Sydney? Was it worth it? Could it happen today?

It is difficult to identify a single causal factor. The struggle connected with general student protest at the time, especially over Australia's participation in the Vietnam War. It was about the omniscience of professors and about academic freedom with respect to the setting of the curriculum. It was about a generation gap between students and younger academics on the one hand and older professors and administrators on the other. It was about inspirational versus pedestrian teachers, about a shared cause, a social network, drinking and partying, and idealism. It was about the core issues and the dominant paradigm in economics. It was about what should be taught to a large number of undergraduate economics students, many of whom were conscripts. It was about strong personalities who were welded inexorably into adversarial positions.

Why did it happen only at Sydney? It is difficult to say why these events appeared to be peculiar to the University of Sydney. Were students elsewhere more accepting, less questioning of their curriculum? Were other courses more pluralistic and encompassing of the interests of staff and students? Were issues of curriculum more readily resolved through consultation and cooperation? Why did the events at Sydney advance much further than elsewhere? Perhaps there was a more radical student and staff tradition at Sydney and the PE struggle was part of an ongoing tradition of dissidence within the University.

Was the struggle worth it? It consumed time, resources and emotional energy. Irreconcilable enmities were established, as were long-term bonds and friendships. Careers suffered, as did many personal relationships. A separate PE course was established, a vibrant and coherent PE group survives today and the *Journal of Australian Political Economy* still serves as a good resource for non-mainstream research and critical analyses of contemporary social and economic policy. A second generation of teachers, students and researchers has carried forward the PE tradition (see, for example, the work of Dick Bryan, Gabrielle Meagher and Stuart Rosewarne). In these terms it was worth it, but it did come at a cost to many on both sides of the debate and struggle.

In addition, many of those at the forefront of protest activities over thirty years ago are now in respected positions in commerce, government and academia. Ironically, some of yesterday's radicals are today's conservatives, even reactionaries. Perhaps for them PE is best forgotten or put down to youthful naiveté. At the same time there were those who were nominally conservative and respected academic citizens who were galvanised into dissidence by what they saw as injustice and intolerance.

Students are now more conservative and career minded, so it's questionable as to whether such a struggle could happen again. The economics discipline is more fragmented and pluralistic in terms of research and teaching. Economics is even less respectable today since it is seen as too abstract and irrelevant for the dominant teaching programs of business and related studies. There is no comparable student protest movement, despite enduring national and international social injustices. Universities are more managerialist in their organisation and goals, and with this the power of professors has become subservient to corporate objectives and professional managers. PE would be allowed today as long as it was profitable, could be taught offshore in Singapore in a one-week sandwich program, contributed to the organisation's research and institutional profile, and presented numerous photo opportunities for corporate managers to pose with benefactors, publication launches and student prizewinners.

I sustained some long-lasting friendships from those events, notably with Evan Jones, and for that I am grateful. I would also mention Frank Stilwell as a model teacher and researcher who still manages to amaze me with his energy, his published output and his perseverance in highlighting the failures of contemporary economic and social policy. The struggle gave me a greater appreciation of the need to recognise that the economics discipline is not monolithic and has a multitude of paradigms, none of which has a superior claim to being correct. Students can be sustained by lecturer enthusiasm, and courses need to demonstrate some relevance towards a better and critical understanding of the world. Finally, while the focus has been on the University of Sydney it is worth emphasising that the PE group has provided a teaching and research agenda for many others to follow. I look forward to the golden jubilee of political economy and to the retrospective evaluations, fireworks and celebrations.

Figure 2. The view from within: political economy student demonstrators in the Quadrangle, seen from inside the administration building (photo from the University's Archives).

1
Emerging conflict

The origins of the political economy dispute at the University of Sydney were local and specific, but reflected the broader political economic conditions of the time. These conditions were conducive to the assertion of ideas challenging conservative orthodoxies.

Support for progressive social changes was growing in Australia in the late 1960s and early 1970s. Opposition to the war in Vietnam and to Australia's part in it, including opposition to military conscription, took hundreds of thousands of students, trade unionists and other citizens onto the streets of all the capital cities, particularly Melbourne and Sydney, and some regional cities and towns. Conservatives and right-wing libertarian members of the Australian Association for Cultural Freedom attempted to neuter this opposition on university campuses but their red-baiting strategies backfired, producing disquiet among people who may otherwise have remained uninvolved. Campus politics had developed a tradition of involvement in wider social and political concerns by the late 1960s and early 1970s. This paralleled the increased levels of industrial struggle and working class confidence that were evident in the post-Menzies period.

The prospect of a change of national government also contributed to a more optimistic view of the possibilities for more progressive public policies. Hopes for a change were given a boost when, in 1972, the Australian Labor Party's campaign to win federal government ended twenty-three years of Liberal-Country Party rule. The new government, under Whitlam's leadership, immediately ended conscription and completed the withdrawal of Australian troops from Vietnam. In 1973 and 1974, before the global recession of 1974–75 set in, other significant policy initiatives followed, including the introduction of free tertiary education, which opened the door to university for a broader cross-section of Australian society. The mood among those of a progressive reformist disposition in Australian universities was relatively buoyant, even though Whitlam's government had its critics on the left as well as on the right. Students felt themselves newly capable of bringing about change in the social order.

The buoyancy also reflected international influences. In the late 1960s there had been dissent in many universities around the world, most famously in Paris and Berkeley. The authority of received wisdom—of hegemonic texts and 'god-professors'—had been challenged, and students were demanding exploration of less conventional modes of learning. On economic issues in particular, there was a renewal of Marxist thinking that coalesced with the development of the New Left in the broad sphere of politics. With the rejection of the Soviet Union's domination of communist parties in most Western nations, including Australia, the tight hold of official Marxism had been broken: rethinking a modern Marxian project became a focal point for vigorous intellectual activity. Locally, the Green Bans movement in Sydney showed the practical possibilities for the labour movement and community action groups to directly confront the power of corporate capital and a corrupt state government. It was a time when an array of radical and dissident views could get a hearing and have influence.

Recurrent themes in the flowering of critical thinking in the universities included the recognition of social classes, accompanied by compassion for the poor and powerless, an interest in the capacities of socialist planning, a commitment to national liberation struggles that sought to combat monopoly capitalism and neo-imperialism, a recognition of environmental and social limits to economic growth and a belief that class analysis should be augmented with an understanding of gender-centred patriarchy. All of these concerns, and more, found expression among dissidents at the University of Sydney in the late 1960s and early 1970s.

The dispute in the Department of Economics that developed within this historical context focused particularly on different views about what constitutes a good education in economics within university teaching. As with any discipline, economics can be taught in various ways. Although some economists think it appropriate to reproduce the prevailing orthodoxy, others regard that orthodoxy as fundamentally flawed and emphasise the need for more critical enquiry. These competing views have important ideological and pedagogic dimensions.

During the 1960s, the Department of Economics' curriculum had emphasised an eclectic mixture of microeconomic and macroeconomic analysis, the latter influenced by the contributions of John Maynard Keynes, and the study of practical features of the Australian and international economies. 'Descriptive economics', the title of one of the compulsory course components (albeit tangential to the theoretically-based syllabus), was indicative of the dominant orientation towards institutional, rather than mathematical, approaches to the subject. It was this curriculum that two new economics professors, Colin Simkin and Warren Hogan, sought to change. Simkin had previously been a professor of economics at the University of Auckland; Hogan, who had been one of Simkin's students before coming to Australia, had obtained a PhD at the Australian National University and had taught at the universities of New South Wales and Newcastle. These two professors were appointed at the University of Sydney in rapid succession—Hogan in

1968, Simkin the following year. Both were chosen by selection committees chaired by the Vice-Chancellor, Professor Bruce Williams, formerly professor of economics at the University of Manchester. These three people were to be central to the turmoil that erupted and persisted on the campus through the following decade.[10] Confronting them, from a position of much lower institutional status, were the dissident students and staff who challenged their authority and decisions.

With the tacit approval of the Vice-Chancellor, Professors Simkin and Hogan set about restructuring the courses in the Department of Economics. Their declared aim was to modernise the department in order to create, they claimed, a more rigorous undergraduate training in the subject. As Bruce Williams stated in his memoir, '[t]hey took the view that the course should be directed more than in recent years to the creation of competent economists and therefore to require a more numerate approach'.[11] What this meant in practice was heavier doses of standard microeconomic and macroeconomic theory with a more mathematical orientation. Under these new arrangements the study of economic policy and of institutional aspects of the relationship of economy to society became more marginal. The first year course (which would these days be two introductory, semester-

---

[10] It is pertinent to note that the Chancellor of the University during the period when the political economy dispute was developing was also an economist. The largely ceremonial position was held by Sir Hermann Black (after whom Hermann's, the student bar in the Wentworth Building, was later named). Urbane, personally conservative and renowned as a public speaker, he was also a senior lecturer in the Department of Economics. As Chancellor he chaired the Senate, the University's formal governing body, but otherwise played no visible role in the emerging conflict.

[11] B. Williams, *Making and breaking universities: memoirs of an academic life in Australia and Britain 1936–2004*, Macleay Press, Sydney, 2005, p. 103.

length 'units of study') had previously provided a general overview of economic issues and analysis: this was replaced by a new Economics I that focused exclusively on microeconomic theory and quantitative methods. Economics II became dominated by macroeconomic theory. Only when they had been schooled in the mainstream principles would students be permitted to pursue a broader array of subject areas in applied economics.

The nature of the syllabus changes and the heavy-handed manner of their introduction antagonised many of the department's existing academic staff, some of whom decided to leave for jobs elsewhere. Those who stayed included Ted Wheelwright, Geelum Simpson-Lee, Margaret Power, Hugh Pritchard, Maurice Haddad and Louis Haddad, all of whom were critical of the ways in which Professors Hogan and Simkin exercised professorial power. Simpson-Lee, for example, was, without prior consultation, relieved of his responsibility for running the Master of Economics degree. Ted Wheelwright wrote to the Vice-Chancellor in 1970, calling for an official inquiry into the department. Ironically, some new lecturers, hired by Hogan and Simkin to teach in the reconstructed courses, readily aligned themselves with these older critics of the new regime: these newcomers were Debesh Bhattacharya, Gavan Butler, Frank Stilwell and (a couple of years later) Evan Jones, all young economists with orthodox economics training and PhDs from universities overseas, and with growing interests in alternatives to mainstream economics. Other newly-hired lecturers of more conservative inclination aligned themselves more closely with Professors Hogan and Simkin. Personal relations among the staff were tolerable, even convivial at times, but an undercurrent of conflict was already evident.

Meanwhile, student discontent was growing. This was more than the usual grumbling about boring lectures in a notoriously dry subject. Students have traditionally put up with these features of an economics education—at best because of the expectation that the courses would eventually equip them to understand how the economy works, at worst because the courses were a compulsory component of a degree that derived its value from its other components, such as accounting and political science.

The new undergraduate program at the University of Sydney evidently did not meet even these modest expectations of the students. The core components, Economics I and II, were seen by many of them as overly theoretical, too mathematical, poorly taught and oriented towards one particular set of economic doctrines to the detriment of a fuller understanding of the real world. Too many unrealistic assumptions seemed to be made, assumptions that required them to suspend disbelief while learning the proffered theories. First-year core microeconomics lectures by Warren Hogan and second-year macroeconomics lectures by Colin Simkin were particular focal points for these criticisms.

A survey of student opinion conducted at the end of 1969 revealed the high degree of dissatisfaction. The head of department, Professor Hogan, responded by impounding the student questionnaires in the following year and terminating the employment of Bill Waters and David Hill, two of the three tutors who had been associated with the survey, when their contracts came up for renewal. The controversial decision not to reappoint these two popular tutors was the focus of a special issue of the student newspaper *Honi Soit* that was published in November 1970. It was the trigger for a series of well-attended protest meetings on campus that continued during the early months of 1971. The repeated calls for the reinstatement of the tutors were to no avail. After working as a builder's labourer Bill Waters eventually got another job, teaching HSC economics at Randwick TAFE. David Hill moved out of tertiary education, later becoming an adviser to New South Wales Premier Neville Wran (working in tandem with Nigel

Stokes, another former lecturer in economics who had quit the University of Sydney in the early 1970s), then becoming, in succession, the chief executive of the State Rail Authority in New South Wales, the managing director of the Australian Broadcasting Corporation and the head of Soccer Australia.

Discontent among students continued throughout 1971 and 1972, even though Hogan had personally ceased lecturing in Economics I and passed the task on to other lecturers, including Frank Stilwell, who tried to teach the subject in a more accessible way. Simkin continued to present the lectures in macroeconomics within Economics II, speaking to usually sparsely populated lecture theatres.[12] Proposals for changes to both the undergraduate and postgraduate curricula were put to departmental staff meetings, but their consideration was frustrated by the lack of democratic decision making, with the result that the meetings became increasingly fractious.

One early illustration of how the battle lines would be drawn arose at the July 1971 departmental staff meeting. Responding to the criticisms of mainstream economics, Simkin requested Stilwell—together with Ted Wheelwright, Gavan Butler and Maurice Haddad—to consider

---

[12] Warren Hogan's retrospective views on this problem are disarmingly understated. He concedes that 'Simkin's teaching was best tuned to individuals and smaller groups. While throughout his career he participated in lectures to large groups, with the passing of the years he had a less sure grip on his audience. This reflected in some measure an inability or unwillingness to adapt to the changing needs and qualities of his students and the requirements of the degrees which they were pursuing': J.E. King (ed.), *A bibliographical dictionary of Australian and New Zealand economists*, Edward Elgar, Cheltenham, 2007, p. 252. The attempt by Hogan to blend a kind but realistic assessment contrasts with Peter Groenewegen's claim that Simkin was 'an excellent and generally well liked and admired teacher', *University of Sydney News*, 25 March 1999.

the possibility of a course in Radical Economics for 1973. The report prepared by the four economists and presented at a subsequent staff meeting argued that the radical challenge to mainstream economics should be considered in all courses, not hived off to a separate elective. It was a strong demand that was quite unpalatable to the two professors but the authors of the report were starting in their own lectures to practise what they preached.

Some of the students were also beginning to make the case for a more pluralist education in economics that would have more direct relevance to understanding the real world. In February 1973, three of them—Steve Keen, Richard Fields and Greg Crough—mounted a radical economics conference to focus on the critique of mainstream economic analysis.[13] This was a significant initiative, although the conference attracted only a small number of participants.

Many more turned up to hear the Nobel-prizewinning American economist Paul Samuelson when he spoke at the University during his Australian visit in March 1973. This was a chance to hear and consider the views of perhaps the most prestigious living economist. Samuelson had spoken elsewhere about the radical challenge to economic orthodoxy that was developing in the USA and internationally, providing his own rebuttal of the dissidents' arguments. Many students and staff at the University of Sydney would have been interested to hear him on that theme. Instead, influenced by Professor Simkin who chaired the event, Samuelson talked on an abstract topic in mathematical economics that was neither interesting

---

[13] In his submission to the 1973 inquiry by the Faculty of Economics into the political economy dispute, Ted Wheelwright noted that 'This was originally intended as part of orientation week, but as the head of department insisted that, if this was to be the intention, he must personally vet any contributions by academic staff, the proposal was dropped. The conference took place independently in February, and several members of staff participated.'

nor intelligible to most of his audience. It was as if this distinguished economist were illustrating the very problem with which the dissidents were concerned. When he started his lecture, the largest lecture theatre in the Merewether Building (where the Faculty of Economics was located) had been packed; by the time he had finished it was nearly empty. Student activist Richard Fields was one of those who stayed, leading the discussion after Samuelson's presentation by asking him a penetrating question about why he had chosen not to speak about the radical challenge to orthodoxy and also, rather impressively, pointing to a problem in one of his mathematical equations.

More significant developments occurred during the second term of 1973. A dispute in the Department of Philosophy arose because of a proposal to introduce a course in feminism.[14] That department had been in turmoil during the previous year because of professorial opposition to an elective on Marxist philosophy. Similar opposition to the new feminist proposal led to a strike of some students and staff; and people in other departments joined the strike to support the new course. The students in Economics I, then being taught by Stilwell, voted to join the strike, as did the students in some other third-year Economics electives. Professor Simkin, who was then Acting Head of Department, was furious, and wrote to Stilwell demanding to know why 'for two weeks your own Economics I classes recently, and with your concurrence, did not have normal lectures but, instead, discussion of issues involving university government as well as the problem in the Department of Philosophy'. Students started to see the parallels between the problems arising from the exercise of professorial power in the two departments. Steve Keen issued a leaflet

---

[14] In the Faculty of Economics a new interdisciplinary elective on the Political Economy of Women, proposed by Margaret Power, was accepted in 1973 and taught for the first time in 1974.

headed 'Economics students: the Philosophy dispute is relevant to you'; and Richard Fields wrote an article for *Honi Soit* on 'The effect of the Philosophy strike in economics'.

Then came the 'day of protest'—perhaps the single most important event in launching an ongoing student-staff movement for political economy. The decision to hold it was taken on 10 July 1973 when a meeting called to address 'the problem in economics' packed out the same large lecture theatre in which Samuelson had spoken. Students at the meeting resolved to organise a whole day of protest activities to draw wider attention to their concerns. Staged on 25 July, this day of protest was supported by about 200 students who boycotted their usual lectures to attend a series of discussions about alternatives to

Figure 3. One of the earliest demonstrations; students marching outside the Merewether Building with the Madsen Building in the background.

orthodox economics. Warren Hogan, who was Head of Department again by this date, wrote to the dissident staff, requiring they give their normal lectures, but many did not comply. During the next few weeks students and dissident staff—calling themselves the Day of Protest Committee—got together to prepare proposals for substantial reform of the undergraduate curriculum. Grumbling about the *status quo* was replaced by the exploration and advocacy of a preferable alternative.

By this stage the dissidents were starting to call their alternative vision 'political economy', a term that emphasised the diversity of ways of interpreting economic issues and the inherent interconnectedness of economic issues with social concerns and political judgements. It was a direct challenge to the dominant neoclassical theory and to the claim by mainstream economists to be conducting value-free enquiry. The dissidents thought micro and macro theory should be studied, but so too should Marxian and institutional economic perspectives. They argued that more attention should be given to contemporary concerns such as economic inequality, environmental degradation, imperialism and the use of economic power. These themes were reflected in the alternative curriculum proposed by the dissident staff and students. Not surprisingly, Professors Hogan and Simkin rejected the proposal, which they saw as a challenge to their authority as well as to their views on economics. They defended the more orthodox curriculum by asserting the priority of core theory, the importance of a supposedly 'positivist' methodology and the need to focus on the key economic issues as represented by articles in the mainstream professional journals. The polarisation between the positions of the professors and the dissidents intensified.

To his credit, Professor Hogan did agree to meet with the students to publicly defend the position he and Simkin had taken. The meeting, convened by the charismatic and increasingly assertive economics student, Michael Brezniak, was held in the Professorial Board Room

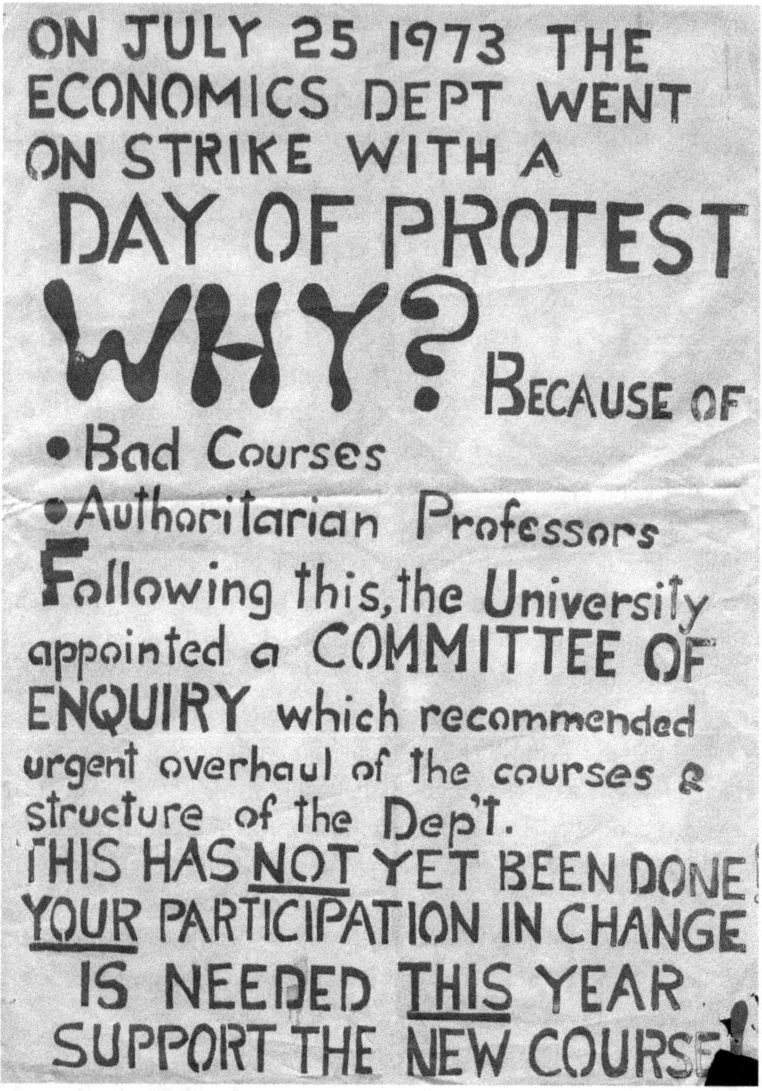

Figure 4. 1974 poster.

on 7 September 1973. Hogan listened to criticisms from Brezniak, Steve Keen and others of the economics courses and the top-down processes of decision making, but would not agree to course reform or to a survey of student and staff preferences. In a subsequent leaflet, reporting on the meeting, Keen described the discussion as 'not so much beating your head against a brick wall as firing bullets into a blob of jelly'.

The leaders of the students' Economics Society (SUES) decided afterwards to conduct their own survey of student attitudes. A questionnaire circulated in all economics classes asked for students' comments on whether they found the various courses interesting or uninteresting, well presented or badly presented. 'Prof Simkin tops poll' was the ironic headline of the article Keen wrote for *Honi Soit* reporting the results of the survey. The questionnaire also sought students' opinion on whether they preferred the current structure of economics courses or the new course structure proposed by the Day of Protest Committee: only eight per cent indicated the former, while eighty-one per cent preferred the latter, the others being undecided.

How was the institution to respond to the polarised positions that had become so evident in the Department of Economics? The economists themselves could evidently not agree on a resolution of the conflicts over curriculum, staffing and decision making in the Department, so a resolution would have to be sought through other channels.

In the first instance this meant intervention by the Faculty of Economics, which comprised academic staff in the Departments of Economics, Economic History, Economic Statistics, Accounting and Government and Public Administration (hereafter referred to as the Department of Government, which was the common abbreviation until this department's name was changed in 2000 to Government and International Relations). Geelum Simpson-Lee, a quietly-spoken senior lecturer in the Department of Economics, had been elected as dean of the Faculty in 1972. As dean, he was in a position to initiate faculty intervention into the ongoing departmental conflict.

The Faculty voted to set up an official inquiry at its meeting on 10 September 1973. Simpson-Lee invited Pat Mills, a reader in the Department of Accounting, to chair the committee; the Faculty endorsed his recommendation and determined that the committee should also include Rex Mortimer and Ken Buckley, associate professors in the departments of Government and Economic History respectively, and two undergraduate students, Graham Kerridge and Stephen Irons. This committee composition ensured that the critical views of the dissidents would get a good hearing. The outcome was no foregone conclusion though. The committee's chair, Pat Mills, was personally quite conservative (one of the last to wear an academic gown while lecturing) and renowned for his independent, judicious approach to faculty matters.

After careful deliberation and consideration of submissions from the interested parties, the faculty committee chaired by Mills issued a thirty-nine-page report. It noted the different views about the nature of economics as a discipline. It also noted 'the deep and bitter antagonisms within the department' arising from the two professors' assertion of their right to determine the curriculum, standards of examinations and allocation of staff duties without consultation with the sub-professorial staff (or contrary to their advice).

The principal recommendations of the Mills report were that a separate Department of Political Economy should be created, staffed in the first instance by the dissident group in the existing Department of Economics; and that those staff should put on courses that exposed students to the diverse currents of economic thought. These recommendations recognised that the professors in the Department of Economics would not agree to modify the existing core courses to accommodate the teaching of political economy. The legitimate

War of the economists

By GAVIN SOUTER

IT IS NOT often that academic strife reaches the stage of seeming able to tear a faculty apart. But when it does, as now in the Department of Economics at Sydney University, the bitterness and waste of time are awful.

Sydney University has had this sort of strife before — notably in its Department of English, over Dr Leavis's peculiar brand of literary criticism, and more recently in Philosophy, over the teaching of Political Philosophy.

In each case hostilities were limited, and did not affect the rest of the Faculty of Arts. Professor G. A. Wilkes routed the Leavisites, and Professor D. M. Armstrong was only too glad to hive his dissidents off into their own Department of General Philosophy.

The trouble at the Department of Economics, which, of course, is in the Faculty of Economics, concerns the teaching of Political Economy. Political economists tend to describe their conventional colleagues as apologists for the status quo — what Karl Marx called "the scientific representatives of the bourgeoisie."

Committed to such "real world" issues as inequality and under-development, they see conventional economics as a sort of medieval scholasticism, obsessed with the question of how many angels can stand on the head of a pin, or rather how many equations can be harnessed to an econometric model of the economy.

In their turn, many of the conventional economists regard their unruly colleagues as [...] [...] probably immune to economics. They think Political Economy is closer to politics than to economics.

But there the parallel with Philosophy's recent schism ends. Dissidents at the Department of Economics, supported by majority votes of the faculty as a whole, want to teach courses in Political Economy and preferably in a new Department of Political Economy alongside such other faculty departments as Economics, Government and Public Administration, and Accounting. This is more easily said than done.

The opposition to Political Economy starts with the department's two full professors — 45-year-old Warren Hogan, who is head of the department, and 59-year-old Colin Simkin; both New Zealanders, and one a former student of the other. Their supporters, with reservations in some cases, are Associate Professor Peter Groenewegen, Associate Professor Jim Wilson, and two senior lecturers: Dr Sol Kim, a South Korean economist who is now an Australian citizen, and Dr Neil Conn.

Professor Simkin is on sabbatical leave at Oxford. That is not a bad place to be, for Sydney's Faculty of Economics, housed in Merewether Building on City Road, is in an uproar. Indeed, it has been

Mr G. Simpson-Lee

Professor W. Hogan

Dr F. Stilwell

Professor E. Wheelwright

DISSIDENT ACADEMICS PLAN 'OUTRAGE' DAY AT SYDNEY UNIVERSITY

in little else for the last four [...]

"Does your Economics course help you to understand the world about you?" asks a student poster in City Road bearing the likeness of a young woman with a sub-machinegun, presumably Patty Hearst. "Or does it hide behind artificial boundaries? For an Economics which opens your eyes and doesn't blind you, support the Department of Political Economy."

This week, nine dissident members of the Department of Economics sent a statement of their case to every member of the university's academic staff.

The nine signatories included Associate Professor Ted Wheelwright and three lecturers: Dr Frank Stilwell, Dr Gavan Butler and Dr Evan Jones. While it is true that there are no conservatives among the political economists, and no Marxists among the Hoganites, the political spectrum on each side is somewhat wider than one might expect.

While Professor Hogan supports Liberal Party economic policies that he signed an academic statement on inflation for Mr Snedden, but was quoted favourably by the ALP in 1972, Dr Conn is presumably persona grata with the present Government (he was sent overseas for the man-

irrelevant, departmental politicking and the wider field of university politics.

Professors Hogan and Simkin came to the department in 1968 and 1969 respectively. Although Professor Hogan has done applied work for Government and industry, both he and Professor Simkin are regarded by the political economists on their staff as the perfect embodiment of what Carlyle once called "respectable professors of the dismal science."

Oddly enough, the dismal science was then called Political Economy. It was not until the 1890s that economics dropped the "political" tag as evidence of its wish to eschew the value judgments which latterday political economists would now like to see espoused again.

Economics was going to be as value-neutral as, say, astronomy, seeking only to measure and analyse. Indeed there is something almost astronomical about those elegant multi-equation models of the economy which econometricians construct so lovingly.

Econometricians measure economic qualities and relationships, and from algebraic models they attempt to anticipate what is going to happen next. The Reserve Bank, for example, uses an 80-equation computerised model of the Australian economy to predict

ist theory, political economy of women, and power and conflict. The third subject (men) in the present course is a series of eight lectures in Professor Wheelwright's elective third-year course in the history of economic thought.

Political economists say that the compulsory core subjects in Economics I and II, as they stand now, are sternly and unnecessarily technical. Economics I consists mainly of Micro-Economics, plus some mathematical method. Economics II is mainly Macro-Economics, with a choice of one course from a list of options. Only in Economics III, which is not compulsory, does the course broaden into international economics, plus two options.

"You kill bright minds with too much technique too soon," says Professor Wheelwright, who once studied under Galbraith at Harvard, and is generally reckoned to be a likely candidate for any Chair of Political Economy. "I tell them, 'You're all spanners and pipes, and no houses'."

Mr Simpson-Lee feels that too much emphasis in early lectures on economic techniques, rather than economic problems, while perhaps being useful to the few students who will become professional economists, is inclined to dampen everyone's interest. "Remember [...]

Theatre was hardly visible for paper darts."

Professor Hogan defends emphasis on technique, and criticises the proposed PE course for its lack of this in the first two years. "Let's face it," he says, "if you're going to look at economic policy you've got to be able to measure things and have some sense of numbers."

In a statement last month to a meeting of faculty, presided over by Mr Simpson-Lee, Professor Hogan criticised the proposed PE course for being too varied in first year ("the outcome could not be the acquisition of understanding in any depth as so much would have to be covered in a limited time"); for lacking clarity about what techniques and statistical competence would be called for; and for reflecting only part of the international debate on political economy, the part most commonly handled in Government or Political Science.

With particularly strong support from the Department of Government, this faculty meeting endorsed the PE courses by 26 votes to 10. The full membership of the faculty is about 100, but they had been approved in principle at an earlier meeting by 41 to 12. At a subsequent faculty meeting last week, one of Professor Hogan's supporters, Dr Ian Sharpe, moved that a committee be set up to consider the transfer of Government from the Faculty of Economics to a new Faculty of Social Sciences.

The motion was lost by 12 votes to 13, but the idea of moving Government and the political economists out of the faculty may be explored further, at a higher level of university authority. Such a move would have no attraction whatever for political economists or the Department of Government.

The faculty approved course is now before the Professorial Board. Another request for a separate Department of Political Economy (passed at an earlier faculty meeting by 34 votes to 19) will be waiting for the Vice-Chancellor, Professor Bruce Williams, when he returns to work after convalescing from a recent operation. The Vice-Chancellor will probably have the final say on this matter, and he happens to be an economist himself. For that matter, so is the Chancellor, Sir Hermann Black.

Does this add up to affinity with the political economists? Perhaps, though most of the political economists doubt it. To their way of thinking, a more important question is whether the decision should rest with a Vice-Chancellor at all, particularly one who is an economist. This is where university politics enter the picture. Who should decide what is taught: the departmental head, the faculty, the Vice-Chancellor, or the Senate?

In an unprecedented move, the Faculty last year appointed a committee to inquire into the Department of Economics. This committee recommended the teaching of PE courses,

Figure 5. The *Sydney Morning Herald*, Saturday 20 July 1974 (extract reproduced with permission).

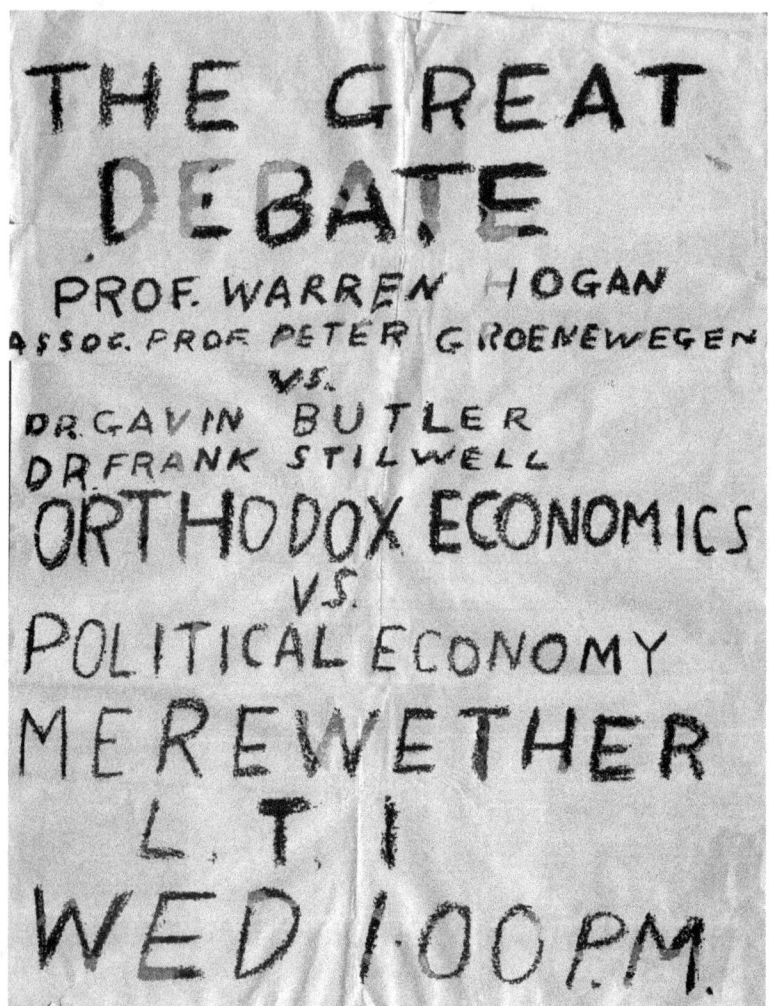

Figure 6. 1974 poster.

interest of students and staff in studying and teaching political economy would require the Department to be partitioned and a new sequence of undergraduate courses to be introduced.

When the Faculty of Economics subsequently debated the recommendations of the Mills committee there was, predictably, strong disagreement. The professors of economics were supported by all the other professors in the Faculty, as well as by some other academic staff, in opposing the proposed political economy courses. They argued that such courses would undermine the professional standing of the BEc degree and enable students to avoid studying 'real economics'. Few of them had made submissions to the Mills committee but they now circulated papers that were strongly critical of its report. Other academic staff, particularly in departments such as Government and Economic History, generally favoured the committee's proposals, arguing that the political economy alternative was legitimate and would otherwise continue to be suppressed.

The Faculty resolved by majority vote (thirty-four to nineteen) at its meeting on 19 April 1974 to endorse the recommendations of the Mills committee. Professor Hogan had tried to head off this outcome with an '11th hour' proposal for minor course changes and the establishment of a departmental committee to review the subjects currently offered. He also accepted the students' invitation to a public debate on orthodox economics *versus* political economy: he and Peter Groenewegen debated Butler and Stilwell in front of some 300 students in the largest Merewether Lecture Theatre on 3 April. However, the positions taken by the defenders and critics of the *status quo* had polarised: the 'war of the economists', as the *Sydney Morning Herald* later described it, had gone too far for effective compromise.

Seeing a naked emperor: Steve Keen

Prominent political economy student activist in the 1970s; now Associate Professor of Economics and Finance at the University of Western Sydney and author of the influential 'Debtwatch Report'.

Like many of those who became involved in the political economy struggle at the University of Sydney, I began as a believer in what I simply thought was economics. There is a first-year tutorial paper, hopefully long lost, in which I bemoan the existence of both monopolies and trade unions.

Such naiveté did not last. In late 1971, Frank Stilwell drove an intellectual bulldozer through it with an untimely illustration during a first-year lecture on the theory of the second best (in a proper economics education, such things are really best left to graduate school when the few survivors are fully committed to neoclassicism). Learning about this wrinkle on the seemingly flawless neoclassical skin shook my world view substantially (with a little bit of help from the Vietnam Moratorium Campaign). So, after signing on for a vacation job, the second thing I did was to join the union.

The following year, along with a new-found radical friend Richard Fields, I organised (if that is the right word) a radical economics conference. It was attended by only a handful of people, with the Henry George League making up a sizeable fraction of the audience and only Bruce McFarlane providing any real intellectual spark.

As my gut feeling disgust for economics grew, I became progressively more disillusioned with economics and with the bulk of my fellow students, who seemed to tolerate this bunk (though nonetheless they, like me, chatted away all through Professor Simkin's incredibly boring second-year macroeconomics lectures). Attempts to challenge the staff on the hidden assumptions of economics met with friendship from a minority who would, sometime later, form the nucleus of the Political Economy Group in the Department of Economics, but outright hostility from the majority. It seemed that this mediocre hegemony—that I now knew to call 'neoclassical'—would dominate economics forever.

All that changed in 1973, when the Department of Philosophy at the University of Sydney initiated a strike over the University's refusal to endorse a new subject, Philosophical Aspects of Feminist Thought. As then president of the Arts Society (my degree was arts/law, not economics) and therefore an *ex-officio* member of the Faculty of Arts, I took an active role in this at both official and street protest levels; the vigour of the students in the Department of Philosophy was a welcome contrast to the passivity that characterised their colleagues in economics.

All this changed when Gavan Butler informed me that students in Frank's first-year economics lecture had voted to strike in sympathy with the philosophy department. The aura of passivity had only been one of resignation: like me, many were fed up with the pseudo-numerate nonsense that permeated our subjects, and we leapt at the chance to do something to change it.

A lunchtime meeting, entitled 'The problem in economics', drew over 450 students. We ranted, with little direction, until Richard Osborne, a previously unknown student in government courses, sprang to his feet to suggest that we should organise a 'day of protest'. Over ten per cent of the audience volunteered to help and, as a result, the political economy student movement was born.

The Day of Protest was a huge success from the moment that fellow student Bill Nicol's 25-metre banner was strung out across the Merewether Building. The adrenalin rush of the event gave our protest a momentum that pushed through a faculty vote to investigate the affairs of the Department of Economics. In response to a challenge from Professor Hogan to 'do better' if we didn't like the current syllabus, we also developed an alternative economics curriculum that eventually became Economics I(P). And, though we didn't appreciate it at the time, we gave birth to a tradition of student activism that, while it has waxed and waned, has lived on for over thirty years—a remarkable achievement.

Looking back on those days from my current position as an associate professor of economics and finance, I feel we did only one thing wrong. Because so much of neoclassical economics is dressed up in sophisticated mathematical dress, we wrongly identified mathematics and rigorous analysis as being at least part of the enemy. Today, I realise that it was not real mathematics but appallingly bad mathematics that clothed this naked emperor of the social sciences. Of course, it remains true that much of economics cannot be put into mathematical form, as Hugh Stretton's *Economics* makes clear with its plea for 'barefoot economists', but truly rigorous mathematics demolishes neoclassical economics, while modern mathematics and computing offer the possibility of a truly dynamic economics that can, at least partially, explain the behaviour of the unstable economic system in which we live.[15]

More than thirty years on, it is still an uphill battle to develop that real economics. The majority of economists still fall prey to the seductive ideology of neoclassicism, while only a handful of the perhaps twenty per cent of academic economists who are non-neoclassical have the intellectual armoury needed to develop an alternative. They struggle on with limited funding while comparative abundance is wasted on those who continue to push the prevailing paradigm forward.

So is the PE struggle ultimately futile? No. We know so much more now about the deficiencies of neoclassical economics than we knew thirty years ago, and economic circumstances today give us the opportunity to shake the hegemony, as Keynes tried to do seventy years ago. With the financial crisis now in full flight, we can now move from merely poking fun at the naked emperor to arguing, with today's living history as our proof, that neoclassical economics is a dangerous delusion that does damage to capitalist economies in the guise of defending them. We need an empirically-based, realist economics, and the struggles over political economy at the University of Sydney long ago were an early Spring towards that objective.

Unfortunately, as Keynes's own experiences during the Great Depression confirmed, true change in economics comes not during the economy's Summer— when the delusion that a market economy is self-equilibrating takes flower—but during its Winter.

---

[15] In his submission to the 1973 Faculty of Economics committee of inquiry into the political economy dispute, Ted Wheelwright wrote: 'It should be noted that mathematics *per se* is not the issue. Most students nowadays have adequate mathematics, and for those who do not, there are courses available. Some of the most rebellious students are at least as well-equipped, mathematically, as many of their teachers ... the objection is the trivialisation of mathematical techniques for their own sakes, without producing conclusions of consequence relevant to the world the students live in.'

2
Getting started

When the Faculty of Economics voted in 1974 to endorse the recommendations of the Mills committee, it paved the way for the introduction of new courses in political economy. After much political lobbying, lively debate and nail-bitingly close voting outcomes at faculty meetings, the way had been cleared for the introduction of an alternative to the mainstream economics courses. The dissidents, having failed to get the professors of economics to agree to major course reform, had been given a green light to proceed with their own courses and the Faculty had recommended that they should have a separate department.

Big hurdles still had to be cleared. First, the Faculty still had to consider specific course proposals before they could get the endorsement required by the Professorial Board—the higher academic authority on which all the University's professors were represented. The political economists decided to go with the curriculum that had been designed jointly by the dissident staff and students after the 1973 day of protest. The first-year course proposal emphasised a pluralist introduction to the types and functions of economic systems, the principal competing approaches to the analysis of the capitalist system—neoclassical, Keynesian, Marxian and institutional—and their application to the study of current political economic problems and policy issues. The second-year course, as originally proposed, was based on an array of electives including the state in modern capitalism, Australian capitalism in the world economy, history of thought in political economy and the political economy of development and underdevelopment. At its meeting on 4 June 1974, the Faculty approved, in principle, the structure of these courses and outline proposals for a full three-year sequence (what would now be called a 'major') and a specialist fourth-year honours program in political economy.

When the Faculty decided to accept these new course proposals it did so despite strong objections from Professor Hogan, who argued there was 'chronic overlap' between the existing and proposed courses, and from other economists, such as Peter Groenewegen and Ian Sharpe. Those critics were out-voted when the Faculty resolved that the proposed first- and second-year courses—Economics I(P) and Economics II(P)—would satisfy the requirement for the compulsory economics component within the BEc degree, which was the only undergraduate degree offered by the Faculty at that time. Formally, the courses would have to be taught by the voluntary labour of the political economists because no new lecturers would be hired; but the Faculty resolved, again by majority vote, to 'invite the head of the Department of Economics … to make departmental resources available for these courses'.

It was a 'cliff-hanger' moment. The Faculty of Economics had approved the new courses, but they would not go ahead unless the Professorial Board endorsed them. And the Vice-Chancellor had yet to say whether he would create a separate department of political economy to ensure their proper resourcing and administration. The two issues—new courses and a new department—were clearly interdependent. The August meeting of the Professorial Board noted that only course proposals that are supported by the relevant head of department would normally be considered, which seemed to effectively rule out the possibility of the Economics I(P) and Economics II(P) proposals being approved. Unless the Vice-Chancellor created a new department it looked like the recommenddations of the Faculty of Economics could not be implemented and the aspirations of the political economists would be frustrated.

Responding to this difficult situation, the ten staff of the Department of Economics who wanted the new courses sent a circular to all the other academics in the University in early July to explain their concerns about the continuing obstacles to the introduction of the courses and the limited power of sub-professorial staff. This, of course, was in the days before email, so the circular (to over 1000 people) had to be reproduced on a roneo machine (old-fashioned manual technology, predating the use of photocopying), folded into envelopes and then sent through the internal mail system. It required a whole weekend's work.

The students had more direct action in mind. They resolved to hold another day of protest, similar to that which had taken place on 10 July 1973. This one, held on 24 July 1974, was billed as a 'day of outrage'. The terminology—and the imagery on the posters promoting the event—had connotations of the violent 'days of rage' initiated by the Symbionese Liberation Army activists in the USA. University security was on alert. Indeed, the mood among the student activists was becoming distinctly more militant. Hundreds of students boycotted their usual classes in order to attend alternative lectures and discussions on controversial economic and political issues, and a lunchtime demonstration in the courtyard of the Merewether Building called on the Vice-Chancellor and the Professorial Board to approve the new course proposals and create a new department. Some of the students marched from Merewether to the Vice-Chancellor's office chanting 'political economy now' and 'resolve or resign'.

The Vice-Chancellor Bruce Williams was unmoved. When he eventually made his views known, in September 1974, he rejected the arguments for creating a department of political economy. He stated that, because there was no clear distinction between the subject

Figure 7. Poster for the 'day of outrage', 1974.

matters of economics and political economy, there was no sound basis for institutional separation. He had the power to create a new department (a power he had implemented in dealing with the similarly intense conflict in the Department of Philosophy) but he decided not to use it in this case. No doubt his own views, as a former professor of economics, and his consultation with the professors of economics shaped his (in)action. His written defence of his position also stated his view that the Professorial Board should not make a decision on the proposals for Economics I(P) and II(P) 'until the department has done so'. This showed a remarkable reluctance to recognise how dysfunctional departmental decision-making had become. Williams sought to defend his position at a special meeting of the academic staff in the Department of Economics on 25 September: he was given a polite hearing but can have been left in no doubt about the political economists' deep dissatisfaction with the position he had adopted.

Meanwhile, the chair of the Professorial Board sought to find a more practical solution to the impasse on the course proposals. He convened a special meeting of the Board with students and staff from the Department of Economics. This was unprecedented. Not all the academics attended but students came *en masse* to Merewether Lecture Room 5 which they decked out with protest banners pinned to the walls. They presented a petition signed by 1400 students, calling for the recommendations of the Faculty of Economics to be implemented. The Board was subsequently provided with further information that it had requested from the Faculty of Economics. Responding to criticisms, the political economists also modified their earlier proposal for Economics II(P), making it into a more coherent single course focusing on the national and international economies, rather than the series of 'short course' electives they had earlier proposed. At its next meeting, in October, the Professorial Board voted to approve the Economics I(P) and II(P) courses.

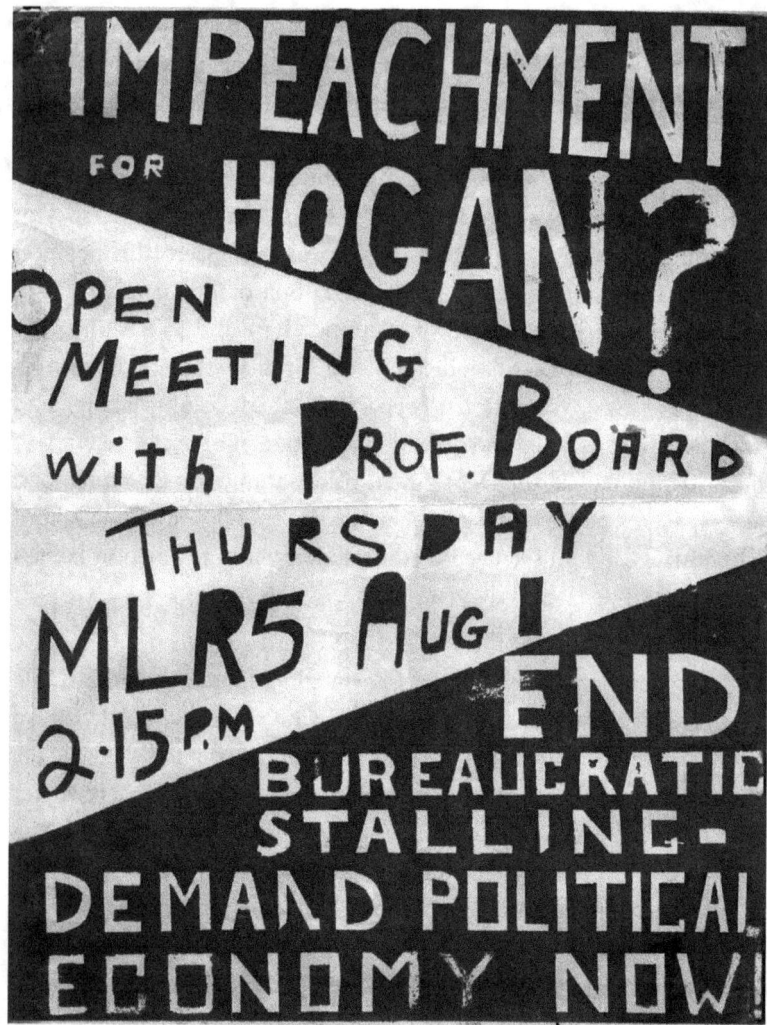

Figure 8. 1974 poster.

So the way had been cleared for political economy courses to be introduced in 1975; but the courses would be formally under the direction of the head of the Department of Economics—a position alternating between Professors Simkin and Hogan, both of whom who had consistently opposed the new courses. This was widely seen as a recipe for further conflict.

Perhaps the tension could have been alleviated by some democratisation of the Department. This view was expressed by fifteen of the academic staff in the Department of Economics—all the political economists plus some other lecturers and tutors—when they petitioned the professors of economics to allow the position of departmental head to be elected by the academic staff. A similar petition in the Department of Government and Public Administration caused its head to step aside. In the Department of Economics, however, there was no such response. The continued assertion of professional power would not be deflected by democratic initiatives.[16]

The power was used in a very direct manner in 1974 when the professors announced—on 28 December—the termination of employment of two tutors, Paul Roberts and Jock Collins. Both had spoken at public meetings on campus in support of the students' demands for course reform. They had feared the sack at the end of the previous year but, now that the new political economy courses had been approved, they expected to be involved in teaching them. After making his case to the Deputy Vice-Chancellor, Collins was given a partial reprieve, being allowed to stay for another year while he finished writing his Master's thesis. Roberts had to go right away.

---

[16] The professors of economics frequently asserted that their power was written into their employment contracts. Professors in other departments sometimes did the same. It is hard to know what to make of those claims because, in the Department of Economics, the contracts were never tabled as evidence.

This targeting of vulnerable tutors on short-term contracts looked like a re-run of the earlier sacking of Hill and Waters, the main differences being that there was now an already deeply-concerned student-staff movement and political economy courses to teach. On campus, concern about the dismissals of Roberts and Collins was widespread and was expressed in *Honi Soit* articles as well as student protest meetings at the start of the 1975 academic year. The ten dissident staff in the Department of Economics signed and despatched a leaflet to all academic staff in the University—another weekend's work—protesting the sacking of Roberts and raising other concerns about the continuing abuse of professorial power. When the Vice-Chancellor responded by challenging the authors of the document to provide evidence of that abuse of power, Butler and Stilwell sent him a confidential document of over 2000 words, setting out chapter and verse.[17]

A mass meeting at the Merewether Building was held on 12 March to protest Roberts' dismissal. Immediately afterwards a group of students continued the demonstration outside the Vice-Chancellor's office. Finding that the Vice-Chancellor would not come out to meet tham, some of the students then went to a lecture theatre where they thought Professor Hogan was teaching, in order to present him with their demands. However, Professor Hogan had invited a visiting professor from the USA to address his class on that occasion. When the protesting students entered the lecture theatre a heated exchange of words between Hogan and student leader Michael Brezniak ensued. Brezniak was subsequently suspended for having disrupted the lecture.[18] This suspension further inflamed student protests. Many

---

[17] They had responded to the Vice-Chancellor's call to 'put up or shut up' but no response from the Vice-Chancellor was then forthcoming.

[18] There is a small error relating to this point in the otherwise excellent memoir of Ken Buckley, who chaired the University's proctorial panel dealing with the

students signed statutory declarations to say they had also disrupted the lecture; but only Brezniak was subjected to disciplinary action.

Responding to the pressure from the activists and the adverse publicity that the University was getting, the Vice-Chancellor agreed to speak publically about his view on the political economy dispute and the Roberts' dismissal in particular. The meeting was held on 20 March in the Stephen Roberts Lecture Theatre, where about 300 students and staff listened with growing frustration to his defence of the current situation. Afterwards, some students, led by political economy activist Rod O'Donnell, followed the Vice-Chancellor back to his office overlooking the Quadrangle, pleading with him for a more positive response. Others, bent on more direct action later that day, spray-painted an area outside the apartment building in Mosman where Professor Simkin lived. It was an act of vandalism that was not consistent with the general concern of the political economists to keep the focus on campus concerns, but the fact that it happened at all was indicative of the intensity of feeling among some increasingly militant student activists.

Meanwhile the new Economics I(P) course had begun. Professor Hogan's written advice to new students contemplating the choice between Economics I and I(P) at the start of 1975 had included the prejudicial statement that the latter would be suitable for those 'with no real interest in economics'. Journalist P.P. McGuinness wrote in *The National Times* that students graduating from the study of

---

suspended student (Ken Buckley, *Buckley's! Ken Buckley; historian, author and civil libertarian: an autobiography*, A&A Book Publishing, Leichhardt 2008, p. 269). Buckley refers to student protests about the subject matter of lectures given by foreign guest speakers, but that was not really the issue in this case because the students had gone to confront Professor Hogan, not his guest, on that day.

Figure 9. Poster for public meeting with the Vice-Chancellor, March 1975.

political economy 'would be qualified in nothing'[19]. Regardless, 316 students enrolled in Economics I(P). A further 86 took the transitional course called Economics II(P) Conversion that was designed for second-year students who had already completed Economics I and who wanted to switch to political economy: these students took the Economics I(P) lectures plus a special 'top-up' of additional material. That means that, in 1975, there were over 400 students in the new political economy program, compared with 393 taking the standard Economics I. The Economics I(P) and II(P) Conversion lectures were presented by the dissident staff within the Department of Economics who had formed themselves into the Political Economy Group for this purpose: Ted Wheelwright, Gavan Butler, Frank Stilwell, Debesh Bhattacharya, Evan Jones, Margaret Power, Geelum Simpson-Lee, Louis Haddad and Jock Collins.

The introduction of the new courses in political economy alongside the mainstream economics courses was the first time any Australian university had offered economics students such a choice. It did not diffuse the conflict in the Department of Economics, however. Relationships among staff in the two camps remained cool, with periodic outbreaks of hostility. Some felt themselves uncomfortably caught in the middle. Tensions arose during student enrolment sessions when staff from mainstream economics and political economy gave conflicting information and advice to prospective students. Department of Economics staff meetings, usually held about four times a year, were characterised by strong verbal exchanges. Professors Hogan and Simkin continued to oppose proposals for further courses catering for the needs of third-year and honours students interested in political economy. In this they were supported by Associate Professor Peter Groenewegen and by other non-

---

[19] *The National Times*, 24–29 March 1975.

professorial staff who either shared their views about the nature of economics and the appropriate syllabus or felt it wise to conform. Groenewegen went along to Jock Collins' opening lecture in Economics I(P) on Marxist economics, and sat conspicuously in the middle of the front row, accompanied by his burly friend David Clark, creating an intimidating situation for this young tutor's first lecturing experience.

The problem of discrimination was also becoming a particular concern for the staff in the Political Economy Group. Geelum Simpson-Lee, as dean, sat on the promotion committees for all applicants from the Faculty of Economics but the committee's decisions were usually dominated by the professors of economics and by a conservative professoriate more generally. Frank Stilwell and Evan Jones both wrote articles for *Honi Soit* about the difficulties faced by the political economists when applying for tenure and promotions. The matter was also formally raised with Professor Geoff Harcourt from the University of Adelaide, then president of the Economics Society of Australia and New Zealand, and with the newly formed Council for Academic Freedom and Democracy in Australia (CAFDA). Extensive dossiers documenting alleged instances of discrimination were presented as supporting evidence.

The rejection in May 1975 of Associate Professor Ted Wheelwright's application for a vacant chair of economics was a particular focal point for allegations of discrimination. This rejection came, ironically, in the same month that Wheelwright was given substantial funding by an Australian businessman and the federal government to set up the Transnational Corporations Research Centre at the University. Wheelwright had also recently sat on two federal government committees of inquiry. As a public intellectual, as well as a teacher and author, he was without peer in the Faculty of Economics. Protest meetings supporting Wheelwright were held on the campus, and a petition calling for the selection committee to reconsider its decision was signed by 116 of the academic staff. However, the University authorities held firm to their decision.

This was a remarkable constellation of concerns—the Roberts sacking, the Brezniak suspension and the Wheelwright rejection—occurring at the very time the first political economy course began. Concurrently, Hogan and other mainstream economists were circulating papers critical of the proposed further development of political economy courses. A petition from 261 students stated their wish to do Economics III(P) but Hogan refused to allow consideration of it at a departmental meeting in April. When Professor Joan Robinson from Cambridge spoke at the end of that month on the intellectual basis of the political economists' challenge to orthodox economics the large Wallace Lecture Theatre was full. The political economy dispute was the most controversial issue on campus, with no end in sight despite the first of the alternative courses getting off to a good start.

By this stage, some of the students studying political economy had become highly effective activists. In addition to Steve Keen, Michael Brezniak and Rod O'Donnell, they included Angela Nanson, Kathi Peterson, Bruce Lanahan, Martin Hirst, Linda Walters, Kevin McAndrew, Rod Pickette, Steve Burrell, Sally Edsall, Alan Madge, Bill Nicol, Rick Kuhn and Clive Hamilton. Others regularly involved in both the political and social activities included Chris Smith, Darryl Hood, Valerie Maiden, Ian Collins, Kathy Thornton, Jude Ellis, Michael Joyce, Mark Openshaw, Lorraine Phillips, Chris Phillips, Steve Vineberg, Mike Kobetsky, Derek Sicklen and Dinah Cohen (who is the central figure on this book's front cover image).

They drove the movement for the further extension of courses in political economy, for adequate staffing and for administrative

Figure 10. Student activist Kathi Peterson addressing a Front-Lawn meeting 1975.

arrangements that would protect the courses, staff and students from what they regarded as obstructionism by the economics professors and their supporters. Several noisy demonstrations occurred. The most notable was that on 2 July 1975 when, following a rally on the Front Lawn and the burning of an effigy representing professorial power, political economy students and their supporters occupied the Vice-Chancellor's office. Bruce Williams was at a Reserve Bank board meeting downtown at the time and, after returning, he authorised

Figure 11. Students dancing around a bonfire on the Front Lawn, burning an effigy representing professorial power, July 1975.

Figure 12. Students inside the Vice-Chancellor's office, July 1975.

calling the police to evict the students. They left peacefully although, from then on, the issue of 'cops on campus' was a major bone of contention for the student activists.

Nurturing activism on campus and beyond: Martin Hirst

Political economy student activist in the 1970s; now associate professor in the School of Communication Studies at Auckland University of Technology.

I arrived at the University of Sydney at the beginning of 1975 to start a degree in economics on a New South Wales Teacher's Scholarship. One of the first people I met was Steve Burrell, a fellow Westie and passionate advocate for political economy, who is now a senior financial journalist for the Fairfax Group. When I met him, Steve had been on campus a few days already.

Steve was on the PE stall during O-Week and convinced me to change my enrolment from Economics 1 to Economics 1(P). Not that I needed much convincing. As well as my working-class background, my mother worked for a trade union. Once I realised there was a choice between orthodoxy and deviance I knew where I stood. I'd been a radical at school, but more rebel without a cause than revolutionary.

My political activity began on my first day as an undergraduate student when I took part in a march across the campus to demand the implementation of the Mills committee recommendation that political economy become a stand-alone department within the Faculty of Economics. I quickly found myself absorbed into the movement which felt like an intellectual and spiritual home. I knew what we were doing was right and I wanted to be in the front lines. So I made sure I was.

I was part of a group that can be described as the second wave of student militants at the University of Sydney: too young to actively participate in the anti-Vietnam Moratorium but certainly influenced by its exciting actions and slogans. I was also drawn to the ideals of the movement and the freedoms won by my slightly older peers in their revolutions of the late 1960s. The second wave was a new layer of activists, many drawn from working-class backgrounds and the first in their families to attend a university. We were the beneficiaries of the Whitlam government's opening up of higher education through the abolition of fees and the introduction of more scholarships. Importantly, we were not bound to the traditions of the New Left and, as part of our education, were being exposed to a range of leftish ideas, from Marxism and Marcuse to the French and Italian poststructuralists. Since then I've always been a Marxist and have tended to ignore the fads.

At the beginning of 1975, the core activists around political economy were the same students who had participated in, and led, the Vietnam protests, the women's movement, the anti-Springbok demonstrations and the black rights protests of the late 1960s and early 1970s. But many new students became willing foot soldiers for the PE movement. It didn't take long for this younger cohort to develop its political ideas and organisational skills. The leadership of the older experienced students, Rod and Carol O'Donnell, David Patch and many others, accelerated our activist education. As well as doing political economy, many of us were also enrolled in philosophy subjects and whatever radical courses we could find in the government department. This new wave of students took centre stage at many events over the next two to three years. For a while this new, second wave broad Left also controlled the SRC, often in uneasy alliance with the ALP students. Eventually, the political faultline between the first wave and the second was over a strategic issue for the movement: should we persevere with the proper channels, or did we need to move outside them into more militant forms of direct action?

In 1975, the activity of the PE movement stepped up. There was now a group of students who openly and proudly identified with political economy. Organising meetings were huge, there were weekly poster runs to do and long debates about theory and politics. In May 1975, we protested outside the Professorial Board meeting. Our demands were for the PE department to be established and for Ted Wheelwright to be given the chair in economics. According to a newspaper report at the time, the beleaguered Whitlam government became involved. 'Left' Senator Arthur Gietzelt called for an inquiry in the non-appointment of Wheelwright on the grounds of discrimination.

The point, really, is that the movement had called in favours from politicians and tried to get the issues dealt with through the proper channels and it had again been rebuffed. I think that the second wave students, now seasoned activists after the campaigns of first term, then decided more militant tactics were needed. I don't know exactly where the idea for an occupation came from, but I was certainly in favour of doing it by July 1975, just six months after arriving on campus.

I don't know why I was so prepared to do something I'd never done before when we occupied the Vice-Chancellor's office the first time. I guess, in today's hip jargon, I was in the moment. Whatever it was, I remember the thrill of hammering away at the doors, one by one with my boots. I can't remember who was supporting me. But we broke the locks and pushed our way past the security staff; the second door was harder, but we got in. I remember being in the office for a couple of hours and intense arguments about going or staying. The police came in, someone read the riot act to us and we left as a group. I don't think anyone was arrested.

Should we have stayed in Bruce Williams' office when the police came? Perhaps, on reflection, yes, but I have not yet reconstructed fully the discussions that were had on the day. To have a purpose, occupations must be carefully considered as long-term actions. A short and sharp protest can make a quick point, but student strikes, like workers' strikes, need to be determined in order to win. During a strike that extends for more than one day an occupation can become an organising base, a union headquarters and a place to rally new recruits.

In the history of the political economy movement we see constant tension between militant reformism and class analysis. In terms of praxis it is the division between working within the system or trying to weaken it through direct action. I'm one of a small number of former PE students who moved sharply and permanently to the hard Left. By 1977, I was centrally involved in the work of the International Socialists in Sydney, including the Movement of Active Socialists at the University. Twenty-five years later I'm still a political economist, and materialism is my intellectual anchor. I'm also still active on the Left as a member of Socialist Alternative, and still at university, now teaching journalism and communication studies in Auckland.

Figure 13. Political economy student leader Rod O'Donnell chats with the students and journalists outside the Vice-Chancellor's office which the students were then occupying.

3
Resolve or resign!

The Professorial Board responded to the continuing turmoil during 1975—and the media attention the University was getting as a result—by setting up a committee of inquiry into the political economy dispute. The motion to do so was moved by one of the student representatives, Malcolm Turnbull (later to become leader of the Liberal Party in the federal parliament). Turnbull was a student of law, not political economy. He sought to play a mediating role in the dispute, meeting with the Vice-Chancellor and separately with the political economy staff and students. His personal confidence in his ability to resolve the dispute through shuttle diplomacy was not matched by any notable success, but his intervention in moving the motion at the Professorial Board was significant. It led to the establishment of a committee chaired by historian Professor John Ward, also comprising five senior academics from faculties other than Economics and one student.

The Ward committee held twenty-four meetings, at seventeen of which it interviewed participants in the dispute. It received numerous written submissions too. It reported in July 1976, by which time the Professorial Board had been reconstituted as the Academic Board with more representation from non-professorial staff.

The Ward committee's report to the Academic Board sought an even-handed approach, which, predictably, led both sides in the dispute to emphasise the aspects that suited them best. On the one hand, the report endorsed the establishment of the first- and second-year undergraduate political economy courses and accepted the case for the provision of further third-year electives. On the other hand, it affirmed the opposition to the creation of a separate department for political economy because there was no clear separation between the subject matters of economics and political economy. However, it did recognise the need for the provision of necessary staff resources and some degree of administrative independence for the political economy teachers, at least for an interim period, in the interest of more peaceful coexistence with the mainstream economists. Specifically, the committee proposed that a 'unit' of political economy be established within the Department of Economics to provide that partial administrative autonomy.

Vice-Chancellor Williams did not comply with the last of these recommendations, remaining adamantly opposed to institutionalising the political economy program. He sought the views of all the individual academic staff in the Department of Economics about whether they thought that the creation of a separate department of political economy 'would facilitate an early resumption of intellectual discourse'; finding that a majority of staff thought it would not do so strengthened his determination to make no change. In his own memoir, Williams makes much of the count:

> Two saying that it would facilitate an early resumption of intellectual discourse, one that it might, five that the creation of a unit was a precondition for further discussions, two that although it might improve the atmosphere for a while they were opposed on the grounds that once created the unit would be difficult to abolish, seventeen that it would not help.[20]

---

[20] B. Williams, *Making and breaking universities*, Macleay Press, Sydney, 2005, p. 111.

Perhaps the political economy staff made a tactical error in not all replying individually that a split would 'facilitate an early resumption of intellectual discourse' but a joint letter they wrote to the Vice-Chancellor should have left him with no doubt that they thought it a necessary step towards solving the dispute. The bloc vote of the seventeen mainstream economists opposing relative autonomy for the political economists was always going to dominate the count though, enabling the Vice-Chancellor to justify his established position.

It was a strange count anyway. In effect, the Vice-Chancellor interpreted negative responses to his question about whether the creation of a political economy unit would 'facilitate an early resumption of intellectual discourse' as meaning that those staff did not want the unit to be established. The Dean of Economics wrote to him in July, querying the basis of his tally and pointing out that 'opinion pollsters are always very cautious about inferring the answer to a question from the answer given to another'. He also reminded the Vice-Chancellor that on four occasions he had referred to the official position of the Faculty of Economics, recommending the unit as a 'necessary condition for the solution of the problems'.

Even more pointedly, the Academic Board committee chaired by John Ward issued another report, pointing out that 'the committee knew that its findings would not be well-received by those most involved in the political economy dispute' and that 'the answers received by the Vice-Chancellor demonstrate the very attitudes in the Department that led the committee to propose the establishment of the Unit'. It concluded: 'we see no reason to amend our original suggestion for a Unit'. In other words ... just do it.

Figure 14. Martin Hirst pastes the demands of political economy students on the door of Professor Simkin's office in the Merewether Building.

Figure 15. The Chair of the Professorial Board, John Ward, in dialogue with the political economy students near his office.

The Vice-Chancellor's refusal to act as recommended fuelled yet more student protests.[21] Following a Front-Lawn rally attended by about 250 students on 2 July, the demonstration continued outside his office. When he declined to come out to meet the students, some of them decided to occupy a section of the nearby administrative offices. The students damaged an iron grid, put there to prevent entry, and they jostled some administrative staff when pushing past. The sit-in lasted for a few hours but when the students heard the police had been called to the campus they left peacefully. One of the policemen called to evict the students later recalled that

> the briefing us coppers received from our more experienced officers at that time would certainly not have met the required standards of today, and certainly took no account of the reasoning behind the action taken by the students. Indeed, were the truth to be known, my understanding was that a group of student radicals were taking over the University, all of whom, it was alleged colloquially, had questionable parentage.[22]

More direct action followed. Overnight, political economy slogans were spray-painted outside the Vice-Chancellor's residence, Wybalena, the beautiful mansion then owned by the University in the elite suburb of Hunters Hill. Like the spray-painting outside Simkin's residence in the previous year, this act played into the hands of conservatives wanting to turn the issue into one of 'law and order'. It was condemned by student leader Rod O'Donnell in a letter written

---

[21] It is notable that the Vice-Chancellor did act in other departments where he thought internal partition was appropriate. The case of Philosophy has already been mentioned. He split Industrial Relations from Economics. In the School of Chemistry, he created 'small d' departments to minimise internecine warfare.

[22] Letter published in the University of Sydney *Gazette*, no. 2, October 2003, p. 2.

Figure 16. Student leader Rod O'Donnell, (later to become Professor of Economics at Macquarie University) meets the press.

Figure 17. Political economy activists: Michael Brezniak (with megaphone) and Steve Keen; Laurie Ferguson in the background.

on behalf of the Movement for Political Economy and published in the *Sydney Morning Herald* on 19 July 1976.

Three students—Martin Hirst and Lance Baker as well as O'Donnell—were suspended, prior to a hearing by a Proctorial Board, for their part in the occupation (not the spray-painting, the culprits for which were never known). Concerns about these selective reprisals fuelled further protests. At a meeting in a packed Wallace Lecture Theatre, reported at the time to have been attended by about 800 students, a general strike was called. The strike was supported by over 100 staff and 4000 students who boycotted their lectures and tutorials for eleven days in support of the demand for the lifting of student suspensions and the creation of a unit of political economy, as recommended by the Academic Board's committee. Activities during the strike were intense—numerous meetings held, deputations sent to talk to students in courses where lectures were continuing, and daily strike bulletins issued. One political economy student, addressing a history class, was physically assaulted by a lecturer.

It was paradoxical that the year following the introduction of the political economy courses was also a year of such widespread protest activity by the supporters of political economy. The tension between the limited progress on course reform and the lack of any progress on administrative reform was the main underlying problem. The political economy activists thought that the future prospects of the political economy courses were being undermined by the intransigence of the Vice-Chancellor in failing to provide the necessary administrative autonomy. By refusing to create a separate Department of Political Economy, or even a unit of Political Economy within the Department of Economics, Williams was seen as ensuring the continuation of the conflict. 'Political Economy: Resolve or Resign' T-shirts were produced by student activists; many posters with a similar theme also appeared on campus.

Figure 18. 1976 poster.

Support for the political economists came from the Students' Representative Council (SRC), particularly during 1976 when law student David Patch was its president. Indeed, for some years afterwards—with the exception of 1979 when mainstream economics student Tony Abbott was SRC president—support for the political economy movement was a normal expectation within the leadership of student organisations on campus. Many clubs and societies also offered support. The French Society was among those that wrote to the Vice-Chancellor expressing solidarity with the political economy students. The Labor Club and the Communist Club, more predictably, issued numerous bulletins supporting the political economy case. Even Liberal Club newsletters expressed support. The sole exception was the Democratic Club, a hangover from the Democratic Labor Party that had played such a damaging role in splitting the Australian

Figure 19. Graffiti during the strike of 1976.

labour movement in the 1950s and 1960s. Francis Xavier Lane-Mullins, a mature-aged student linked to the Democratic Club and the National Civic Council, also distributed a series of 'independent' newsletters that sought to discredit the movement for political economy with propaganda that was redolent of the 'red-baiting' in the 1950s and 1960s.

The first national political economy conference

About 1500 people came from all over Australia to the political economy conference that was held at the University of Sydney in June 1976. This was a massive show of support for the proponents of political economy at a time when the struggle on campus was particularly intense. The timing of the conference, in relation to national political economic events, was also significant. Three years of Labor government under Gough Whitlam had come to an end when Malcolm Fraser, then leader of the Opposition, and John Kerr, the Governor-General, had contrived its dismissal on the spurious ground that the government could not guarantee the passage of the supply bills necessary to provide continued finance for government payments. This constitutional coup was interpreted by many Australians as a cynical repudiation of normal democratic processes. It contributed to a mood of defiance among the critics of the Fraser government.

The national political economy conference that was held in the middle of the following year tapped into this mood. While that conference was primarily concerned with the critique of mainstream economics and the exploration of political economy alternatives, it also provided a timely opportunity for critical analysis of contemporary political economic events.

The inquiry into the political economy dispute by the University of Sydney's Professorial Board was still in session at the time of the conference. The chair of the committee of inquiry, historian Professor John Ward, chose to interview some of the senior conference participants, including Ed Nell and Geoffrey Harcourt, then professor of economics at the University of Adelaide. Whether they influenced the committee's recommendations cannot be clearly known, although it is notable that the Vice-Chancellor openly responded to some of Nell's arguments and also made use on other occasions of Harcourt's view that radical critics of economics need a thorough knowledge of the orthodoxy first. Undoubtedly though, the presence of internationally recognised political economists at the conference and the strength of local support added to the legitimacy of the political economy movement.

Recollections of traumatic times: Jock Collins

Postgraduate student and tutor in the Department of Economics in the 1970s; now Professor of Economics at the University of Technology, Sydney

In 1971 I graduated from the University of Sydney with an economics degree. Unless I stayed on for further education I would have been conscripted to fight in Vietnam, so I enrolled in a Masters of Economics, with no real idea of what I should write a thesis on, but I was interested in Marxism so I decided to do a Marxist analysis of immigration. At this time I also got a job as a tutor in the economics department.

Being an active proponent of political economy did not endear me to Professor Warren Hogan, the head of department for most of this period. On one occasion, I walked out of a departmental meeting—with Paul Roberts, a fellow tutor and political economy supporter—after I had made a speech about the need to establish courses in political economy. Hogan was livid. Being employed on annual contracts made Roberts and me vulnerable. Rumours soon spread that we wouldn't be re-employed. I still had a year to go on my Masters and had published some book chapters on Australian immigration. With lingering memories of the sacking of Bill Waters and David Hill during my years as an undergraduate, it was beginning to appear that history would repeat itself. Paul and I wrote to then Deputy Vice-Chancellor Professor O'Neil, arguing our case to be re-appointed; we also had a meeting with him about the matter. I was able to convince O'Neil that I should be re-employed for the next year, but Paul was not so lucky: his contract was not renewed at the end of 1974 and, at the end of 1975, nor was mine.

In the life of the political economy movement and for student politics at Sydney University more generally, 1975 was a major year. I had been elected as a student representative to the Faculty of Economics board, from where I witnessed much of the debate. During my first board meeting I sat opposite the economics professors, stupidly staring down Colin Simkin. I became aware of how important this forum was to the future of the political economy movement, which had some supporters in the faculty, particularly in the Department of Government. Frank Stilwell, Ted Wheelwright, Gavan Butler, Margaret Power and Evan Jones carried the fight for political economy at this level. The then Dean of the Faculty, Geelum Simpson-Lee, was also sympathetic to the Political Economy Group. Student support for political economy was growing strongly. Many meetings and rallies were held where we mulled over strategy and tactics. At one stage, after a meeting addressed by Frank Stilwell, myself and student leaders, students occupied the offices of the university's Vice-Chancellor. Martin Hirst and Rod O'Donnell, two student leaders, were suspended. Mindful of my tenuous hold on my job, my role as a sole parent and a thesis deadline that was rapidly approaching, I kept out of this part of the struggle.

In the following year, the political economy strike was a highpoint of activity. The student PE group called on staff and students to strike in order to turn up the heat on the struggle. Together with the PE student leaders, I addressed economics lectures and sought support for our strike. Along with Angela Nanson, a PE student, I was assigned the task of getting Ted Wheelwright's support as well. I thought that would be easy. Ted, even though he was not very active in the PE movement, was its intellectual mentor; the staff leadership fell mainly on Frank Stilwell and Gavan Butler. I remembered seeing Ted on television before going to uni: 'Red Ted', as he was called, played a significant role in the media at the time as an often lone left voice in Australian economic and political debate. Wheelwright had been a great teacher, he and Stilwell were by far the best lecturers I have ever had. Both had an ability to communicate, to interest and to bring enthusiasm to their subject matter. During the meeting in his office, Ted floored me when he said that strikes were outdated tactics unsuited to universities and that he would not support ours. I went home to my (very 1970s) collective household and cried to my friend Hal Alexander about my disappointment of the meeting.

But Ted continued to be a figurehead for the political economy movement. His first volume, *Essays on the political economy of Australian capitalism*, edited with economic historian Ken Buckley, was published in 1975, and a second volume in 1977, both of which I had chapters in. The books filled an important void in the available Australian political economy literature. Ted continued to publish in the area even after his retirement from Sydney University in 1986. It was a scandal that he was never appointed to be a full professor of economics, blocked as he was by the bitterness that permeated the economics department for many years, the opposition of the existing economics professors and the opposition of Vice-Chancellor Bruce Williams, himself an economist. Ted's legacy of scholarship and teaching in Australian political economy provided the intellectual grounds on which his younger academic colleagues could stake their fight against the economics orthodoxy.

Despite the disappointment over Ted Wheelwright's lack of support, the PE strike had some impact. It was used as a forum to broaden student support and to educate students in alternative economic views. We managed to attract newspaper interest, including articles in the *Sydney Morning Herald*; there were also items on ABC Radio's *AM* and *PM*. Pressure mounted on the university and on Williams to resolve the dispute. After a couple of weeks, we decided to call it a day: I had to finish and submit my Master's thesis, while many students turned their attention to mundane university activities such as exams and essays. But the strike was successful in highlighting the case for having political economy subjects in the economics degree.

The introduction of the new political economy courses—Economics I(P) and II(P)—was a bittersweet victory for me. They were to be taught in the year when my employment in the department was terminated. With the help of Harold Levien, I got a job teaching Higher School Certificate economics at Seaforth and Sydney TAFE colleges. I was also employed by the Political Economy Group to teach the Marxist Economics lectures in Economics I(P), which I did for two years. In 1977 I was successful in getting a job as lecturer in economics at the newly formed Ku-ring-gai College of Advanced Education. My new boss was Hugh Pritchard, formerly a senior tutor in the economics department at the University of Sydney, and I worked with him at Ku-ring-gai CAE and then at UTS (after the two were amalgamated in 1989) until his retirement in 2000. I continued my links with the PE movement for a few years after I left Sydney University.

Two things stand out from this time—the first political economy conference and the establishment of the *Australian Journal of Political Economy*. The PE conference, held in 1976, provided a huge forum for Australian research and debates. As with many events in the PE struggle, the conference was accompanied by partying and music. The PE movement was part of a broader cultural movement of the late 1960s and early 1970s—music, dress, hairstyle, alcohol and drugs were central to the cultural and political activities of the day.

Two memories stick in my head from that first conference. One is economic historian Ken Buckley yelling at me over loud music during a party that we should have arranged for some quieter space where older people could continue their discussions while the younger cohort danced. The second is of a moment during the plenary session at the end of the conference when I jumped up from the audience to explain that we didn't want to be known as the Radical Political Economy Movement because political economy had been born of a radical movement and the term was redundant. One of the resolutions passed at this meeting was to establish the *Journal of Australian Political Economy*. I was on the editorial committee of *JAPE* for the first few years, and had the honour to write (with the late Mike Brezniak) the first article in its first issue. The journal continues to this day, largely through the efforts of Frank and other PE staff, including Gavan Butler, Evan Jones and Stuart Rosewarne.

While my formal contacts with the Political Economy Group had ended by the early 1980s, I have remained friends with Frank Stilwell and his colleagues, who continued with amazing stamina and perseverance to fight for the PE course. They were victorious, finally, when the degree of Bachelor of Economics (Social Sciences) was established and the Political Economy Group became a *de facto* autonomous department. We hoped then that this victory would be the vanguard of other institutional challenges to neoclassical economics and the economic rationalism that has dominated the Australian economics profession. I still hope to see more of these challenges to come.

Figure 20. ABC TV crew arrives to film a political economy rally at the University Front Lawn, 1975.

Plate 1. Poster for the conference on radical economics at the University of Sydney in 1973 (organised by economics undergraduates, Greg Crough, Richard Fields and Steve Keen).

Plate 2. Poster for the first national political economy conference at the University of Sydney in 1976. (The conference speakers included Sam Bowles, Edward Nell, Ian Gough and Herb Gintis; the conference was attended by approximately 1500 participants.)

Plate 3. Poster for the political economy conference at the University of Sydney in 1979 (with original graphics contributed by Patrick Cook).

Plate 4. Poster for the political economy conference at the University of Sydney in 1982 (featuring US President Ronald Reagan and Australian Prime Minister Malcolm Fraser).

4
More struggles

Dissent within the Department of Economics simmered for the remainder of the 1970s. The two undergraduate political economy courses—Economics I(P) and II(P)—were running well and enrolments were growing, rivalling the numbers in the mainstream economics courses. The existence of these political economy courses was an opportunity for various forms of progressive educational experimentation, including group research projects, student self-assessment and collective assessment. A weekly meeting ('PE hour') was introduced for talks by visiting speakers on topics of general interest to students. Two groups, each of about sixteen political economy students and staff, went on visits to the People's Republic of China in 1977 and 1978. Political Economy conferences in Melbourne (1977, 1980), Adelaide (1978) and Canberra (1981) were attended by many Sydney students; while another big conference at the University of Sydney (1979) linked the PE staff and student organisers with the concerns of community activists exploring the political economy of 'social control'.

In May 1978, in conjunction with the SRC's Education Action Committee, the Political Economy Students Association organised a week of alternative education with the theme of 'PE: still going strong'. This recreated some of the atmosphere of the earlier day of protest and day of outrage. Alternative lectures, seminars and films were organised. Among the seminars was one on 'Why capitalism stuffs up your personal life', presented by political economy student Ann Harding (later to become Professor of Economics at the University of

Canberra and director of the National Centre for Social and Economic Modelling). Michael Brezniak, Rod O'Donnell and Jock Collins presented special guest lectures to Economics I(P), much to the consternation of Professor Gordon Mills, who had got the third chair of economics instead of Wheelwright and was head of the Department of Economics at the time.

Apart from a general interest in developing political economy as a critique of mainstream economics and a means of understanding contemporary social issues, the main continuing concern of political economy students and staff was the lack of progression in the political economy program. The pragmatic arrangement that had been imposed on the Department of Economics by the Professorial Board in the mid-1970s—two years of Economics 'P' courses that undergraduate students could take instead of mainstream economics—was proving to be unsatisfactory. The situation was not wholly bleak because the Professorial Board had also required the reform of Economics III so that political economy students would not be left wholly 'high and dry'. A series of fractious staff meetings in the Department of Economics during July 1976—five sessions in two weeks taking a total of sixteen hours—had hammered out some minimal changes to meet this requirement.

Third-year students could choose from a mix of short courses and electives that included a couple of political economy options among an otherwise fairly standard set of orthodox economics topics. However, the professors of economics continued to block other proposals from the political economists for electives that would cater more fully to third-year undergraduate and honours students. The result was that the options available to students interested in the political economy approach were severely restricted in comparison with the wider array of mainstream economics electives. Those students interested in taking an additional year to complete an honours degree in political economy faced an even more difficult situation: some switched to other disciplines that were more tolerant of a diversity of social science perspectives, such as Government and Industrial Relations (which was allowed to formally separate from the Department of Economics in 1975).

Staffing issues were also a concern. The political economists' proposals for tutors to be employed to teach in Economics I(P) and II(P) were frequently frustrated: the professors refused to accept the recommendations for Michael Brezniak, Kate Short and Terry O'Shaughnessy to be hired. An attempt to appoint the British political economist Dr Scott Moss as a lecturer was also thwarted. The number of lecturers in the Political Economy Group declined to seven (out of a departmental total of twenty-six), with the result that only twenty-seven per cent of the department's staff was teaching an estimated thirty-seven per cent of the total undergraduate student load. The desire of students for more courses was hard to reconcile with this rising student:staff ratio in the political economy program.

These ongoing concerns about course progression and staffing erupted in further demonstrations in 1981, after the professors of economics rejected a substantial proposal for reform of the third-year and honours courses in economics. Professor Hogan, who had become again head of department, allowed a delegation of political economy students—Greg Spice, Steve Burton, Louise Titterton, Peter Ferris and Steve O'Neill—to attend a departmental staff meeting in June. These students and others had put extraordinary energy into producing a large document, in which they set out the developments they desired. The proposals were further elaborated by the political economy staff at a subsequent meeting but the professors did not find them to their liking. Not only were the proposals rejected, there was also no acknowledgement of the disciplined interest that the students had shown in seeking to develop their own education.

A petition signed by approximately 700 students, calling for more political economy electives, an honours program and better resourcing, was then taken to the Vice-Chancellor. John Ward held this official position now. Ward, who had formerly been chair of the Professorial Board and chair of its first committee of inquiry into the political economy dispute, had replaced Bruce Williams following Williams' retirement in 1981. Students, seeking to present their petition, demonstrated outside Ward's office on 8 September. Ward responded soon afterwards by asking the Academic Board to establish another official investigation into the Department of Economics. This new committee of inquiry was to be chaired by Professor Gerry Wilkes of the Department of English (who had been a central figure in a major split in that department that had occurred in the 1960s[23]) and included four academics from faculties other than Economics and a postgraduate student. As with the earlier committee chaired by Ward himself, this committee conducted extensive interviews and received numerous, sometimes lengthy, submissions during its deliberations in the summer of 1981–82.

The Wilkes committee report, issued in April 1982, noted that 'the (P) courses had successfully accommodated interests that are properly pursued in a Department of Economics, and there is abundant testimony that graduates with this training are valued outside the university'. However, it also noted that little progress had been made towards the resolution of the departmental dispute, that better progression for political economy students into senior years of study was needed and that some new administrative arrangements were appropriate. As a pragmatic step, the committee recommended that one of the political economy staff be designated 'professor most

---

[23] 'Crisis looming in English Department: Wilkes creates new course,' *Honi Soit*, vol. xxxviii, no. 21, 15 September 1965.

concerned' for the courses and be given responsibility for their staffing and administration. This institutional change was intended to enable the teachers of political economy to administer their courses with some independence. The report also recommended that the Department of Economics review its course structures with a view to providing 'freedom of movements and the transfer of teaching expertise from one course to another, instead of institutionalising differences of approach or method'. The sting in the tail was that, if the department could not make substantial progress in this last respect, the Academic Board itself would need to exercise its power to determine the courses.

How would the Department respond? There was a flurry of activity. Numerous staff in the Department circulated papers setting out their preferred 'model' for the economics courses. Some wanted separate streams of political economy and economics courses; others did not. The political economists put up a proposal that would allow for some teaching by mainstream economists in the political economy courses in exchange for further development of political economy electives at third year level. Warren Hogan put up his own proposal for a common course that would have eliminated Economics II(P) as well as I(P). The Vice-Chancellor also made it known, in a statement to the Academic Board on 19 July 1982, that he favoured a common course.

Fearing the loss of Economics I(P) and possibly Economics II(P) too, some political economy students pitched a tent in the Quad and stayed there overnight on 27 July 1982. It was a foretaste of some more militant protests that would occur in the following year.

The SRC got involved, organising a referendum in May 1983 on the proposals for course restructuring. Approximately forty per cent (an unusually large percentage for student ballots) of a possible 1900

Figure 21. 'The Faculty of Political Economy' caravan parked on the Front Lawn of the University in 1983. Note the banner hanging from the main tower which the student activists were occupying at the time.

students in the Faculty of Economics voted, and, of these, eighty per cent voted for the maintenance of separate streams of courses. The response of the economics professors was to question the legitimacy of the opinion-gathering procedure and to speed up the push for a common compulsory syllabus, thereby producing the very outcome that the poll of students had shown to be so unwelcome.

Widespread incredulity among students at the cynicism of this procedure fuelled the demonstrations and occupations that took place in the winter of 1983. On 8 June some students towed a rented caravan into the university grounds and parked it in the middle of the Front Lawn. Adorned with a banner describing it as 'the Faculty of Political Economy' the caravan was used as an information centre for the protest movement. It stayed there for over three weeks, staffed day and night by political economy student activists such as Stephen Yen, Maria Barac and Paul Porteous. The University authorities were strongly displeased by the presence of the protest caravan but it was harassment by college boys that eventually made it unsustainable.

Other audacious acts followed. On 15 June students entered and occupied the clock tower in the Quadrangle. Damage, estimated by the university authorities at $96, was done to the hands on the western face of the clock. Then, on 20 June, student activists blocked the entrance to the professorial boardroom, adjacent to the Quadrangle, where the Academic Board was scheduled to consider what action it would take in the absence of any agreement about course restructuring within the Department of Economics. After the students were prevailed upon to withdraw and the meeting began half an hour late, some of the protesters then climbed onto the roof of the cloisters outside. Here, they made a considerable clamour, chanting and shouting through a megaphone, with the purpose of disrupting the proceedings. Some damage to the slate tiles on the roof occurred. The

Figure 22. Political economy activists, including Anthony Albanese and Paul Porteous, on top of the clock tower.

Figure 23. The view from the clock tower occupied during the protest of 15 June 1983.

university authorities initiated disciplinary proceedings against six activists: David Re, Adam Rorris, Tony Westmore, Daniel Luscombe, Chris Gration and Anthony Albanese (later to become Minister for Infrastructure, Transport, Regional Development and Local Government in the Rudd government) who they identified from photographs taken during these demonstrations.

The Academic Board's ruling of 20 June 1983 was that more courses in political economy at the third-year and honours levels should be permitted, but that the separate first-year course in political economy should be terminated. Instead of students being able to choose between the first year courses, Economics I and Economics I(P), there would have to be a common introductory course. The Academic

Figure 24. Students demonstrating in the Quadrangle outside the Professorial Board Room, 20 June 1983.

Figure 25. Students on the roof of the cloisters, 20 June 1983 (from the set of official photographs taken by the University authorities to identify students for disciplinary purposes).

Board resolved that the political economy staff should teach one term of this new 'combined' course while the other two terms would be taught by mainstream economics lecturers presenting standard microeconomics and macroeconomics.

The new arrangements imposed on the Department of Economics by the Academic Board also recognised that the teachers of the political economy courses were a distinct group requiring some independence from the professors of economics. To achieve that partial autonomy, Frank Stilwell, who had been recently promoted—after two previously unsuccessful applications and an appeal to the Academic Board—to associate professor, was invited by the Vice-Chancellor to be the first director of the political economy courses. The director's responsibilities were formally deemed to be equivalent to those of a professor in a multi-professorial department. However, John Ward drove a hard bargain: for example, he refused to provide the separate secretarial staff that professors were normally given. And, although his decision to create a director for political economy formally acknowledged the identity of the Political Economy Group, it fell short of the long-standing demand for a separate department.

More demonstrations followed. The staff common room on level three of the Merewether Building was taken over for a sit-in by about eighty political economy students on 29 June. The Vice-Chancellor came to Merewether to persuade them to withdraw. He asked Stilwell to negotiate with the activists to ensure his personal safety before he entered the occupied part of the building. Ward was courteously treated during the 90 minute interchange of views that followed, but the students did not leave. They stayed overnight and only departed the following day after he called the police. About thirty officers came, including a contingent of the black leather-jacketed 'tactical response group' who assembled outside Merewether in Butlin Avenue. Faced with this strong police presence, the students decided to leave peacefully. One student, Chris Gration, was arrested after he had been drawn into an argument with a plain-clothes officer who he said made a homophobic remark: the police version was that Gration had kicked the tyre of one of their vehicles and resisted arrest. The University laid its own charges against three more student leaders—Paul Porteous, Marijke Conrade and Maria Barac—bringing the total number facing disciplinary action at that time to nine.

Then, a week later, another group of political economy supporters re-occupied the Merewether common room, this time with a view to a longer stay. The police could have been called onto campus again, of course, but the students had shown their ability and commitment to sit-in (and sleep-in) as often as it suited their cause and they were evidently not cowered by the possibility of further disciplinary action. Ten days elapsed before they eventually called off the occupation.

Figure 26. Political economy students, with Maria Barac at the front, meet with the Vice-Chancellor John Ward (bottom right) during their occupation of the Merewether staff common room in 1983.

Figure 27. Students in the staff common room during the occupation.

Figure 28. Dramatic scene outside the Merewether Building following the occupation.

The students' concerns and activism notwithstanding, the death knell for Economics I(P) had been sounded. The Academic Board's ruling required the academic staff in the Department of Economics to design a new common first-year course.

The committee that was established for this purpose included two staff from the Political Economy Group—Wheelwright and Stilwell—and four other economists—Tony Phipps, Judy Yates, Russell Ross and Murray Milgate—all good teachers with some understanding of the political economists' aspirations. The committee did make some progress during its four meetings, totalling nearly eight hours of discussion, in the next few weeks. However, potential agreement foundered on a seemingly minor matter—whether the political economists' one-third share of the new course would take the form of a distinct term (one of the three terms into which the academic year was then divided). The political economists strongly preferred that arrangement, arguing that it was necessary to ensure the coherence of their contribution and that it was what the Academic Board had already decreed. The other economists on the committee would not agree, wanting the political economists to teach smaller segments in each of the terms and arguing that the overall coherence of the course would be greater if there were more integration of the different sections.

The matter went back to the Academic Board for resolution. By the narrowest of margins (forty-eight votes to forty-seven), the Board opposed the literal interpretation of its own previous recommendation—that is, that the political economists should be responsible for a distinct term within the course. This was a setback for the Political Economy Group. However, the Senate subsequently took the reverse view—that not giving the political economists a separate term would violate the package of reforms arising from the

Wilkes committee report. It ruled that the Board's decision did not comply with the accord that had already been established.

This created a remarkable situation because the University's principal decision-making bodies were at odds with each other. The conflict became yet more evident when the Academic Board subsequently reaffirmed its earlier decision. The political economists then said they would not teach in the course as proposed. The stalemate was not resolved until 17 January 1984 when the Vice-Chancellor ruled that, contrary to the Academic Board's position, the political economists should have their separate term. This ruling, albeit ostensibly on a small organisational detail, enabled the course to proceed and was a significant boost for the morale of the political economists.

The victory was short-lived though. Almost as soon as the new combined first-year economics course had begun the opponents of political economy began meeting to discuss how, having lost the battle, they would try to win the war. The new course lasted for just three years, with Wheelwright and Stilwell teaching the political economy component in 1984 and Evan Jones and Stilwell doing so in 1985 and 1986. In principle, the common introductory course was a reasonable arrangement: it meant that all students had exposure to both mainstream economic theory (micro and macro) and political economy (focusing on Marxian and institutional economic alternatives to the mainstream) before choosing which of the second- and third-year streams they preferred. Indeed, it was the sort of introductory course with which the dissidents would have been quite satisfied if it had been introduced in the 1970s.

However, the professors of economics and their supporters evidently did not like a situation whereby all economics students had a systematic introduction to political economy. It would not be long before they combined to expunge political economy altogether from the BEc degree.

Nor was Vice-Chancellor Ward comfortable with how the fallout from the dispute in the Faculty of Economics adversely affected the University in general. In February 1984, he initiated discussions on possible faculty restructuring. One written proposal he put forward was to shift the Political Economy Group (and staff in other departments, such as Government, who taught courses that many students combined with political economy) to another faculty newly created for that general purpose. Such a shift would have 'purified' the Faculty of Economics and left it centred on (mainstream) economics, accounting, econometrics, economic history and industrial relations. The resolution of the political economy dispute was widely seen as the main objective of the exercise.

The Academic Board's standing committee on academic procedures and organisation (SCAPO) carefully considered the Vice-Chancellor's proposal and other possible organisational models for the restructuring of faculties. Its final report made the case for creating a Department of Political Economy as part of a package of changes but it did not embrace the Vice-Chancellor's notion of a new faculty in which to locate it and the other untidy 'bits' that did not comfortably fit elsewhere in the University (what Ted Wheelwright called a 'cesspool faculty'). Instead, it focused on structural change to the Faculty of Economics itself. The key recommendation was that the Faculty be dissolved and replaced by an interim arrangement: three boards of studies with responsibility for courses in professional economics subjects, social sciences and (from another faculty) social work. The Academic Board's chairman disagreed, putting the case for a more speedy and direct creation of a new Faculty of Social Sciences. A new faculty seemed unlikely to be sufficiently well resourced, however, especially in the absence of any department of sociology. In any case, the staff in the Department of Government were opposed to being relocated in any faculty other than Economics. Consensus on any organisational change proved impossibly elusive.

In the end, all that the Vice-Chancellor's initiative on faculty restructuring produced was evidence of how much the professors in other faculties resented being affected by the negative 'externalities' of the conflict in the Faculty of Economics. The Vice-Chancellor eventually backed away from his own proposal and nothing was done. Yet the flurry of interest in institutional restructuring was a portent of changes that would resurface two decades later—and result in Political Economy and Government being relocated in another faculty.

Developing skills for social change: Paul Porteous

Student political economy activist in the 1980s; subsequently executive director at the Centre for Social Leadership, senior advisor to the president of Madagascar and fellow at Harvard University.

'Police vs Students: Uni Clash' shouted the newspaper banner over a graphic picture of baton-wielding police. That wasn't quite how it was supposed to have worked out. A fleeting newspaper headline, little more than a footnote to the history of the struggle, hid years of hard work, frustration, passion, emotion and incredible learning that characterised being a part of the political economy movement.

Political economy became more than an issue; it was a lifestyle that involved initiating the PE Students' Association, running the regular lunchtime PE Hour, helping organise the annual PE national conference, advising students on orientation day, endless Academic Board, committee, faculty, department and SRC meetings, and the direct political action that stirred the passions. Certainly, the direct student action is what most people remember—from the protests outside the Vice-Chancellor's office, to putting up a tent in the Quadrangle (even having a lecture there), to occupying the clock tower, to sitting a caravan on the Front Lawn for a fortnight, to occupying the Faculty of Economics building. It was fun, and it was a great group of people who had a common sense of purpose and no idea of what would happen next.

Figure 29. Students confront baton-wielding police in 1983 (as depicted by a newsagent's poster advertising the *Sydney Morning Herald*).

There were moments of great confusion, too, when friends became enemies, enemies became friends, conservatives showed themselves to be far more liberal and occasionally, radicals proved themselves to be far more fundamentalist and inflexible. The University administration also played its part in the drama, particularly in providing itself as a wonderful common enemy and displaying a level of intransigence so old-fashioned that it should have been nominated for a heritage award.

There were funny times, such as when university security spent the whole night at the base of the clock tower with a photographer to catch us on the way out, only to learn that we had already left the evening before through a side door. And there were frightening moments, such as the night when college lads violently attacked our protest caravan on the Front Lawn, their college principal casually brushing off the incident as the result of good spirits after having 'just won a tennis match'.

The occupations and subsequent events remain most vivid in my mind, as do planning strategies, organising and building support in order to take action. The feeling of belonging to something special, something different, at times became overwhelming. Quite often the issue itself got lost among our struggle to understand what we actually represented, which went far further than a course at a university.

Those difficult competing issues of purpose and values were put aside as we planned action, often not realising that, once the pressure was on, those differences were going to burst out at the most inconvenient times. Trust is a fragile creature. On the second day of occupying the Faculty of Economics, we were still arguing not just about how to make decisions but also about how to make the decision about how we made decisions—we couldn't get consensus, we didn't want to vote; majorities seemed to leave out a lot of people. How could we negotiate with the University without agreement on a position? Organisations from outside the University were starting to turn up, radical groups with no student affiliations were demanding a voice, student groups from other faculties who also wanted to add their agendas to our demands were joining in. Instead of working on key issues, discussion became more like a political forum; 30-second sound bites became more important than clarity of purpose. We kept reassuring ourselves that direct student action had worked in the past. 'We *can* achieve victory—just look at General Philosophy'. Sadly, the truth was less palatable. Many changes were coming to the University as the result of powerful conservative professors refusing to have radicals in their departments, rather than from a desire to establish a safe house for them.

Law had not been my most exciting subject but suddenly I had an interest in the *Enclosed Lands Protection Act of 1901*, which was being used as the legal instrument to end the occupation. Lectures were being cancelled due to the occupation and, clearly, many students were no longer supporting the action. One evening a graduate student burst into the men's toilets in the Merewether Building with a PE banner he had just ripped down and, in rage, threw it in the latrine. Combine these kinds of activities with the internal group dynamics and it is no surprise that, from the hundreds protesting in the days before, only a handful remained in the occupation by the end. Suspicion, factions and power struggles had taken their toll. Lord of the Flies ruled and we had already imploded well before the University could touch us.

In the wash-up, nine of us were called to account for the disturbances. We were summoned to an inquisition. How many times can you say 'No comment' to a barrage of questions without hearing and feeling the grinding, stifling wheels of bureaucracy and history at play? 'No comment' didn't impress them. A proctorial panel was set up, presided over by the Chief Justice of the District Court and with QCs on both sides. The process unfolded, with us almost as bystanders. Lawyers in full flight argued technical points, expressing mock shock that there were no signs anywhere suggesting students could not protest on the roof of the Academic Board. How was a student to know? Freedom of speech and the right to protest was the real issue—and we lost. In any event, whatever the outcome, the University had just put on a show trial—the suspensions suspended, the potential martyrs denied martyrdom. I appealed, and won that appeal, but by then it was yesterday's issue and everything was already back to business as usual.

On reflection, the real learning from being in the PE movement was about how our society works and what levers can be used to effect change and mobilise people. It was about how to force your agenda, how to keep your issue alive and not be taken out of the game in the process. In practice, that meant taking action with the ombudsman, petitioning the Senate, soliciting the support of unions and journalists, and writing in the University newspapers, *Honi Soit*, the *University News* and *Union Recorder*.

The key was to avoid being distracted from our main aim—and the University tried hard to distract by focusing on technical details, adhering to formal procedures, manufacturing processes, making it personal instead of about the issue and taking disciplinary action instead of addressing the real problem. They were masters at dealing with symptoms and avoiding the issues. So, we all learnt to play the game at multiple levels—the formal structures, the academics, the journalists, the unions, the backroom powerbrokers, the numbers game, the direct student action. Transforming ideas into action—what better lesson could we have ever taken from a course in political economy.

Figure 30. Political economy 'caravan' at the Front Lawn with student activist Stephen Yen sitting outside.

5
A long march

The political economy dispute was less in the news during the period from the mid-1980s to the end of the century. The undergraduate political economy courses had been established, some relative autonomy for the political economy staff within the Department of Economics had been achieved and the enthusiasm of the students for study of the subject continued to be strong. The tradition of regular student and staff consultative meetings, by now well established, was maintained. The three positions for elected student representatives on the board of the Faculty of Economics were usually occupied by political economy students. The economics 'P' courses were running well, with considerable enthusiasm from both staff and students. That said, the situation of political economy in the Faculty of Economics was not one of a steady state, still less of 'equilibrium'. An atmosphere of conflict continued to pervade staff relations, presaging further threats to the political economy program.

The biggest threat came in 1984 from the Dean, Professor Stephen Salsbury, whose personal antipathy towards the political economists had been intensified by the student occupation of the Merewether Building in the preceding year. During that occupation Salsbury had written to Stilwell, urging him to use 'a bullhorn' (megaphone) to instruct the demonstrators to leave. Salsbury, a US expatriate who was politically on the extreme right, had become dean in 1980, three years after he arrived to take up the chair of economic history and a year after Simpson-Lee had vacated the deanship prior to his retirement from the University. The occupation of the staff common room in

Figure 31. Cartoon appearing in the *Union Recorder*, 1983.

Merewether had so incensed Salsbury that he was implacably opposed to the political economy staff and students from then on. It came as little surprise when, in conjunction with the professors of economics, he subsequently moved to marginalise political economy by removing it from the core of the Faculty's principal undergraduate degree.

Salsbury launched a degree restructuring process in 1985. He thought that, although the faculty restructuring discussions in the previous year had not led to political economy being purged from the Faculty of Economics, it could be purged from the BEc degree. The initiative was supported by the heads of all departments in the Faculty. Buoyed by this professorial consensus, Salsbury set up two committees—one for a revision of the existing BEc and another to consider the introduction of a Bachelor of Economics (Social Sciences).

This proposal to create two different degree programs within the Faculty of Economics was highly controversial. Initially, it provoked yet more student dissent and demonstrations. However, the proposed change also provided opportunities. It meant that further political economy course developments could become possible, including honours courses, albeit not so readily accessible for students enrolled in the BEc degree. The political economists participated in the degree restructuring process, reluctantly at first but rather more enthusiastically later when they recognised that there was no feasible alternative.

The committee looking at the BEc degree included the accounting, economics and econometrics professors who were generally opposed to the presence of political economy. Predictably, it proposed that the common Economics first-year course (in which the political economists taught the second of the three terms of lectures) should be disbanded and that the subsequent choice between Economics and Economics (P) streams should be denied. Instead, the core courses in the BEc should become the exclusive domain of mainstream economics. The proponents of this change thereby sought to cleanse the Faculty's principal degree program of any significant 'taint' of political economy. Students wanting to study political economy rather than mainstream economics would have to do so in a new undergraduate degree developed specifically for this purpose, the BEc(SocSc).

The committee to consider the latter degree comprised Associate Professor Michael Hogan (no relation to the professor of economics) from the Department of Government, Ron Callus from Industrial Relations, and Eric Kiernan and Stilwell from Economics. Michael Hogan, who chaired the committee, took a strong leadership role and ensured that a broadly based degree was recommended. But the process of getting faculty agreement to it was extraordinarily fraught. Kiernan, together with Gordon Mills, came up with an alternative proposal for a degree that would have been, in effect, a social sciences 'B stream' without any explicit provision for students interested in political economy to proceed to an honours degree. The voting at a very tense Faculty meeting narrowly defeated (by twenty-eight votes to twenty-two) the Kiernan-Mills proposal in favour of that designed principally by Michael Hogan and Stilwell. Among those campaigning against the latter was Peter Groenewegen who had become head of the Department of Economics. He supported a revised BEc that excluded any remnant of the Economics 'P' courses and opposed the proposal to have two degrees, thereby denying space in which the 'P' courses could be relocated. Old wounds were reopened.

The successful Hogan-Stilwell proposal included a big concession— that half the first-year economics course would be taught by teachers from outside the Political Economy Group. However, when it came to the crunch, none of the economists wanted to do it (other than Groenewegen who nominated himself to take four lectures when the course began in 1987). So the outcome in practice was the restoration of Economics I(P), albeit now only available in a 'second' degree. The key test would be in the marketplace. Would the newly designed BEc(SocSc) degree become attractive to successive generations of students? Propaganda aimed at undermining the legitimacy of the new degree came predictably from Groenewegen's journalist friends McGuinness and Clark and also from former University of Sydney right-wing student leader Tony Abbott (later to become a prominent minister in the federal government led by John Howard). Writing in *The Bulletin*, Abbott noted that Warren Hogan had christened the degree 'Bessie' and ended his article by employing the standard scare tactic about job prospects. Clark, continuing his vendetta, wrote in the *Australian Financial Review* about 'BESSY, a cow of a degree for those who will be virtually unemployable'.[24] However, right from the start, student interest in seeking entry to the new degree was strong. The UAI score required for admission to the BEc(SocSc) degree program rivalled, and in subsequent years sometimes exceeded, that of the BEc degree.

The restructuring of the faculty's degrees created the situation whereby, from 1987 onwards, all students studying economics at the University of Sydney had two possibilities open to them—enrolling for the BEc, with its compulsory mainstream economics and econometrics requirements, or enrolling for the BEc(SocSc) with the choice of doing either mainstream economics or political economy within that degree. It was not a symmetrical arrangement. The mainstream economists insisted that their courses would be compulsory within the BEc, whereas students had the choice between studying mainstream economics and political economy in order to meet the requirements for the BEc(SocSc) degree. In practice students opting for the BEc (SocSc) degree chose overwhelmingly to study political economy. Many students from other faculties, particularly Arts and Education, also continued to take political economy units

---

[24] Tony Abbott, 'Marxists have a Bessie degree,' *The Bulletin*, 21 January 1986; D. Clark, 'BESSY, a cow of a degree, for those who will be virtually unemployable,' *Australian Financial Review*, 9 February 1987.

EDUCATION

Marxists have to settle for a 'bessie' degree

By TONY ABBOTT

ONCE, Sydney University's political economy course seemed to have everything in its favor — radical chic lecturing staff, the reputation among students of being easy to pass and the support of the campus rent-a-crowd. Now, under a new degree structure, Marxist-oriented political economy will still be taught but no longer count as the major component of an economics degree.

Late last year the university Senate gave the Economics Faculty approval to award two degrees for courses commencing in 1987. Bachelor of Economics is reserved for a revised course beefed up with the extensive mathematical and statistical analysis required in financial management. The study of political economy will entitle students to only Bachelor of Economics (Social Sciences) which is unlikely to be regarded as a serious economics degree. Head of the Economics Department and long-time foe of political economy, Professor Warren Hogan, has christened it "bessie."

The term "political economy" once referred to any study which examined economics in society rather than as an abstract science. About 15 years ago a group of young turks in Sydney University's economics department, gathered around Associate Professor Ted Wheelwright, adopted the nomenclature to distinguish themselves from the majority of departmental economists. These, they claimed, were teaching what was stale, unimaginative and irrelevant.

It is conceded that by the late 60s the department was languishing but the proponents of political economy claimed then, as now, that teaching warmed-over Marxism was not the answer. At first they were on the defensive.

In 1975, after a great deal of student unrest, the department agreed to teach two years of political economy and to recognise these courses as alternative core components of the economics degree. While the standard or "orthodox" course concentrated on banking, trade, the role of government in a mixed economy and analytical skills, political economy mostly comprised a critique of capitalism. It was "sold" by its student supporters as "relevant, democratic and critical."

The 70s were marked by vicious confrontation between the radicals and their opponents. Lectures were boycotted and demonstrations staged. On several occasions the office of the Vice-Chancellor was occupied. The struggle was conducted with the spite which characterises academic feuding and which would be familiar to viewers of the recently screened BBC serial *Historyman*.

Both sides became preoccupied with the need to score points and, particularly, to attract students. Inevitably, standards suffered. While the supporters of political economy thrived on polemic, most orthodox economists regarded this as a distraction from teaching and research.

In those heady days the revolution seemed just around the corner — at least on campus. The onset of staff and student militancy in a department usually was followed by an exodus of more conservative staff. But in Economics the radicals struck an opponent with ideological commitment, bureaucratic nous and sheer dogged determination to match their own.

Once an embattled figure who would chain smoke and stonewall through interminable department meetings, Hogan believes the recent changes to degree structure mean the attempt by "Glebe patio intellectuals" to dominate economics teaching has largely failed. Most share this opinion although department members prefer not to speak for the record.

On the record, the Dean of the Faculty of Economics, Professor Steve Salsbury, says there is "more hope than ever before" that the dispute will terminate: "I think both sides realise that we've wasted an enormous amount of time."

According to Salsbury, both sides have won. The Bachelor of Economics (Social Sciences) degree will give supporters of political economy the chance to run a full honors program. On the other hand, the revised Bachelor of Economics degree will ensure that "the label is an honest one."

Salsbury emphasises that political economy has not been "frozen out." It still will be possible to take political economy in addition to orthodox economics. But he admits that the old degree, which allowed a student taking political economy to graduate without the knowledge economists are expected to have, was "not a solid one."

Supporters of political economy have been on the defensive since 1983, when plans were announced to combine the first year of the course with orthodox economics. Because orthodox economists largely had stayed put during the troubles of the 70s and because ceilings had curtailed the recruitment of political socio-political economy staff, two-thirds of the teaching was to be orthodox. In response, student supporters of political economy occupied the Economics Faculty building for three weeks. The occupation alienated many staff. One senior academic commented that the political economy faction "operated like a political party rather than a group of academics."

The amalgamation also seems eventually to have eroded their student support. In 1985 the number studying second-year political economy fell from 252 to 180.

It would be wrong to conclude that students are now more politically conservative but they are more hardheaded. An indication of contemporary student interest is 217 students took Business Economics as a third year option in 1985 but only two took Marxism and Socialism.

Dr Gavin Butler, founder of the political economy movement, says there is no reason to regard the new Bachelor of Economics (Social Sciences) degree a "Mickey Mouse." The anti-mathematical and marxist-oriented approach of political economy has not, according to Butler, jeopardised the job prospects of students.

But how many will be prepared to take that chance? □

Warren Hogan: Glebe patio intellectuals defeated

THE BULLETIN, JANUARY 21, 1986

Figure 32. Tony Abbott's view of the political economy dispute in 1986. Reprinted with permission of the author.

within their degrees. Even some students doing the BEc opted to do a political economy elective or two, over and above their compulsory core courses in mainstream economics. Students seeking professional accounting credentials, or wanting to do business-oriented subjects, were compelled to study mainstream economics though: so too were students studying agricultural economics in the Faculty of Agriculture.

The forced separation of political economy from mainstream economics in different degrees made it possible for the political economists to have Economics III(P) and their own honours program. In this respect they finally won what they had been seeking ever since 1975, the denial of which had been the cause of so much frustration, so many petitions and periodic demonstrations in the intervening years. On the other hand, the mainstream economics courses remained yet more firmly rooted in conventional micro and macro theory with a strong emphasis on mathematical technique. A decade of challenge by political economy had made relatively little impact in the latter respect, although a couple of the staff in the Department of Economics who were interested in the history of economic thought and post-Keynesian economics evidently felt some disquiet about the hegemony of orthodox economic theory. Hiving off political economy to a separate degree had, in effect, diminished the pressure for reform within the mainstream economics courses. It was back to business as usual.

The use of that last expression is somewhat ironic in this context because pressure on mainstream economics education was now starting to come from a different source—the rising demand for business studies. In the 1990s HSC enrolments in business studies surged dramatically, while economics enrolments dwindled. University students, particularly international students, also revealed their strong preference for business and management education.

Typically, they showed little interest in economic theory, taking only those economics courses that were formally required for their degrees (and usually assessing them poorly in course experience questionnaires). Aping the University of New South Wales (UNSW) and seeking to cater to the evident preference for business studies, the Faculty of Economics at the University of Sydney introduced a third degree, the Bachelor of Commerce in 1993. Ironically, this was what some of the political economists' submissions to the earlier Wilkes enquiry had advocated—a separate degree for those whose interests were primarily in commercial and business subjects. Students in the BCom degree had to do fewer compulsory units in mainstream economics than students had to take within the BEc. Their focus was mainly on accounting, commercial law, finance, marketing and human resources management. Enrolments in the new degree quickly surpassed those in the BEc.

This growing emphasis on business studies was—and remains—a tension for mainstream economists. The challenge to economic orthodoxy that had been mounted by the proponents of political economy for the previous two decades was confrontational. The challenge coming from teachers and students in business-oriented subjects for which the abstract micro and macro theories evidently have little practical relevance is problematic in a different way. It cannot be similarly dismissed as ideologically motivated and it has forced economists to consider how to make their subject acceptable—as a service course—to students wanting a practical management degree. This has not been easy for economists wedded to abstract theories. Some commerce-degree students have chosen to take elective units of study in political economy, presumably seeing that subject matter as better serving their need for a broad perspective on current economic issues. Thus the changes in degree structures undertaken during the deanship of Stephen Salsbury produced some unforeseen effects for the relationship between political economy and mainstream economics. The attempt to marginalise political economy, although vigorously pursued, was not successful.

By the 1990s it seemed that the political economy program had become generally accepted within the Faculty of Economics. A range of third-year undergraduate options had been introduced and the fourth-year honours program was attracting excellent students. The PE program as a whole had a reputation for being interesting, challenging and generally well taught, with flexible forms of assessment and cooperative staff-student relationships. Steps had also been taken towards the development of postgraduate studies, with the introduction of a research-oriented Master of Economics (Social Sciences) degree program in 1990 and, in 1999, a coursework Master's degree that emphasised Australian political economy.

Some *de facto* administrative autonomy for the Political Economy Group had also been achieved, although its formal location within the Department of Economics continued to be a source of recurrent tension, particularly in relation to staffing for the courses. Dick Bryan, after holding a fixed-term lectureship in political economy for a couple of years, got the tenurable lectureship that became available after the retirement of Ted Wheelwright in 1986; Stuart Rosewarne, initially hired as a tutor, made the transition to a more permanent position after a long tussle with the economics professors over whether his employment would be continued. The professors in the Department of Economics were reluctant to appoint additional lecturers in political economy, despite growing student enrolments.[25]

---

[25] There was some to-ing and fro-ing within the Department of Economics later in the 1990s. For example, Debesh Bhattacharya left the Political Economy Group, while Joseph Halevi shifted in the other direction. Gabrielle Meagher got a lectureship following the retirement of Margaret Power; and Tim Anderson and Liz Hill both made the transition from associate lecturers (tutors) to half-time lectureships.

The honours and postgraduate courses had been mounted without any new political economy staff positions. The case for a separate Department of Political Economy, first made in the early 1970s, was still relevant twenty years on although the prospect of its ever happening seemed to have faded.

Ironically, even though institutional separation was denied, spatial separation occurred. The political economy staff got a separate building—for two years beginning in 1998. This was the elegant but run-down former University of Sydney Press building that had become vacant after the winding up of the American Studies Centre (no relation to the US Studies Centre set up at the University, with financial backing from Rupert Murdoch, a decade later). Because of the shortage of office space in Merewether, the then dean of the Faculty of Economics, Murray Wells, called for volunteers to relocate to the nearby Press Building. The Political Economy Group, after much discussion of the pros and cons, offered to do so and, undeterred by the administrative complexity that then arose, they were permitted to shift there. It turned out well: there were almost enough offices (a couple of staff stayed behind in Merewether) and having a distinct space created a strong collective identity. The building seemed like a citadel for the political economists. Classes for the newly-established Master's degree in Australian political economy took place there, as did a series of evening seminars on contemporary political economic issues that attracted progressive intellectuals from other departments and universities. Some lively parties were held too. But occupying the Press Building turned out to be a short interlude. After two years, the Chancellor, Dame Leonie Kramer, decided that the building would be better used for another purpose—as a restaurant facility and conference centre. So it was back to the Merewether Building for the political economy staff, now located on the top floor, above the mainstream economists and in rooms formerly occupied by the Department of Accounting.

Figure 33. The Press Building where the political economy staff had their offices between 1998 and 2000.

Meanwhile, a new dean had been appointed in the Faculty of Economics, starting in 1999. He was Peter Wolnizer, already known to some of the older political economy staff because he had started his career in the Department of Accounting at the University of Sydney two decades earlier. He had subsequently held more senior appointments elsewhere, including a stint as Dean of the Faculty of Business and Law at Deakin University in Victoria. Back at the University of Sydney, Wolnizer quickly initiated a general restructuring of the Faculty that, among other things, formally separated the political economy program from the Department of Economics. The separation was part of a broader set of organisational arrangements designed to conform with university-wide requirements. Senior university administrators were then favouring schools, rather than departments, as organisational units: this meant an extra layer in the bureaucratic hierarchy. The BEc(SocSc) degree was also revised and re-launched as the Bachelor of Economic and Social Sciences (with more prominence given to both Government and Industrial Relations).

Wolnizer's bigger plan was to create a 'world class' centre for business and management education. The name of the faculty was changed from the Faculty of Economics to the Faculty of Economics and Business: and it was reorganised into two schools—the School of Economics and Political Science and the School of Business. The former initially comprised five disciplines (as departments were then to be called)—economics, political economy, economic history, government and international relations, and econometrics and business statistics. The latter initially comprised accounting, finance, marketing, transport and logistics management, together with work and organisational studies (a re-badged industrial relations grouping that put increasing emphasis on human resources management and general management issues). It looked like a tidy, symmetrical arrangement. It also created, as a side effect, a separate Discipline of Political Economy, which made the reorientation of the Faculty towards business studies more palatable to the political economy staff than might otherwise have been the case.

Thus Political Economy entered the new century as a distinct administrative unit. The autonomy continually advocated by the political economists and endorsed by the Faculty of Economics when it adopted the recommendations of its own committee of inquiry into the political economy dispute over two and a half decades earlier had been substantially achieved. The necessary conditions for the administration of a coherent and sustainable political economy program seemed to be in place at last. It was a celebratory moment.

As it turned out, the thirty-year struggle for political economy was far from over. Indeed, it was about to enter a new phase, a phase that would be dominated by the fallout from the transformation of the

Faculty of Economics into a more narrowly-focused and professionally-oriented business school. The political economists had got more independence from the mainstream economists but at the expense of becoming more vulnerable to faculty managers who had no more empathy with their academic concerns.

Finding educational freedom and challenge: George Argyrous

Student in the first cohort of students graduating with honours in political economy, now senior lecturer in the School of Social Sciences and International Studies at UNSW

I began Political Economy at Sydney University as an Economics/Law student in 1982. The Sunday before semester began, one of the Sunday newspapers ran an article warning that unsuspecting students were in for a shock; that Ted Wheelwright would give the introductory ten lectures in the first-year PE course and his message was doom and gloom for Australian capitalism. We were indeed shocked—and inspired. I eventually dropped the Law component of my program as I became more engrossed in studying Political Economy.

The early 1980s were exciting times to be a PE student. Nationally, the economy was moving into severe recession, the Fraser government lost office to Labor under Hawke and hopes were high for a new direction in economic policy. Locally, the University administration was in the process of disbanding the first-year PE course, which led to student occupations of the Merewether Building. Along with many others, we took over the staff common room, held impromptu seminars, and held rallies because we believed—rightly as it turned out—that collective action mattered to keeping PE alive.

Fortunately, I was in a very unique cohort of students. At the time, first-year Bachelor of Economics students had a choice between traditional micro/macro or PE as their core subject. In 1982 more students were selecting PE than were selecting the mainstream micro/macro courses. Two years later this choice was removed, I suspect as a result of the popularity of the PE option, so that students could only move into systematically studying PE in their second year. However, the possibility of studying PE in the final honours year was established for the first time and I took advantage of that opportunity to study PE in more depth. With the first-year PE course disappearing behind me but upper level and honours courses opening up in front, I completed four years of PE. Such a complete program of studies in PE was not to be available again until the 1990s.

Reflecting on this period, I am struck by two elements of my experience. The first was the intellectual freedom given by the PE staff to students who wished to pursue their individual interests, and to do so in ways that were unconventional. In first year, I completed a group research project on employee participation in the workplace, involving interviews with managers and union officials. In second year I became interested in Keynes and wrote an independent essay on the 'meaning' of the General Theory; this was overly ambitious, I now realise, but at the time it was a profound intellectual experience.

When I compared my experience with that of friends in the orthodox economics program I was shocked at the sterility of the tasks they were set. And when I went on to postgraduate study in New York at the New School for Social Research I found myself ahead of my classmates because of my background in political economy. Yet PE students at the time were disparaged by the mainstream economists and a number of prominent Australian journalists for being 'unprepared' and incapable of 'solid' economic analysis.

The other outstanding aspect of my experience studying PE was the student cohort of which I was a part. Despite claims that PE graduates would be unemployable, the opposite has turned out to be true. I still keep in 'regular' contact with my fellow PE graduates, in some cases because they have become prominent commentators in the media or elsewhere in public life (including the current federal government ministry). Other members of my small honours group went on to become academics, a businessperson, a union research officer and the manager of Wellington airport (NZ). All of us were passionate about the need to sustain PE as an academic pursuit and to use it for some 'public good'. The political economy students also seemed to be a much more convivial bunch of people than those studying orthodox economics.

6
A significant shift

During their three decades of struggle, the political economists had become used to political opposition. Even after some relative autonomy was achieved in 1983 and the separate degree of BEc(SocSc) began in 1987, conflict continued on a range of matters—staffing and resources, appointment of tutors and numerous niggling matters of departmental administration. However, the orthodox economists who had sought to deride political economy as not 'real economics' had, bit by bit, become less disconcerted by the presence of political economists among the academic staff in the Faculty.

By the end of the century, most of the academic staff in the Department of Economics who had originally opposed political economy courses had moved on. Warren Hogan had retired (eventually) in 1998 and Peter Groenewegen in 2002, while Gordon Mills had long since moved 'sideways' into a Centre for Microeconomic Policy where he continued as the sole researcher. The newly appointed mainstream economists seemed to regard the political economy staff who had offices on the level above them in the Merewether Building as largely irrelevant to their concerns. The opposition now came from a different quarter, was of a different character and was more concerned with the bottom line from a business perspective.

The increasingly instrumental approach to business education stemmed in part from policies towards tertiary education. From 1996 onwards, the Howard government dramatically cut universities' funding, forcing them to vigorously seek alternative revenue sources.

Attracting more international fee-paying students became the main game, and the Faculty of Economics and Business at the University of Sydney was particularly well placed as a big player. Disciplines such as accounting and finance grew rapidly; and new disciplines, such as business information systems and international business, were established. The result was that the School of Business became bigger and better resourced than the School of Economics and Political Science. Within the latter school, the Discipline of Economic History was closed down in 2002. The Discipline of Political Economy was financially squeezed, partly because the number of international fee-paying students who enrolled in political economy was much lower than for the more directly business-oriented disciplines.

There were some growth areas for political economy, though. The introduction in 2005 of a new degree, the Bachelor of International Studies, attracted a surge of good students to the study of political economy. Political economy became a compulsory core subject within that degree (along with units of study from Government and International Relations). This was not because the dean or head of school sought to give political economy that central role. Rather, it was the consequence of the mainstream economists declining to modify their course sequence to fit in with the objectives of the new degree: they insisted that students would have to take the standard microeconomics and macroeconomics units of study before they could study the international economy. The political economy staff, by contrast, were more inclined to offer directly relevant units on international economic and financial issues. The head of school gave approval for a new lecturer in the Discipline of Political Economy to be hired for that purpose, and Dr Bill Dunn was appointed to the position.

The staff in the Discipline of Political Economy also responded to the increasingly commercial imperatives within the Faculty of Economics and Business by mounting new units of study within the Faculty's postgraduate business degrees. From 2003 onwards, they taught units on topics such as international trade regulation, corporate codes and supply chains, the rise of China, business regulation in Southeast Asia, and relations between the global economic power blocs of USA, Europe and Japan. Impressive enrolments of fee-paying students were initially achieved. The political economists also responded positively, albeit with initial qualms, to the proposal by the head of the School of Economics and Political Science that they teach two of the electives in the Discipline of International Business concerned with the management of risk. Student enrolments in those two electives numbered in the hundreds and included many international fee-payers, but the Faculty of Economics and Business never made the expected financial transfers to the Discipline of Political Economy for doing the teaching. Looking back at this experience, it is hard to avoid using the term 'swindled'.

The dean also declined to provide funds to replace political economists who retired—Dr Gavan Butler and Dr Pamela Cawthorne (in 2004) and Associate Professor Evan Jones (in 2005), all three of whom shifted after retirement into honorary positions as research associates. A prodigious growth of new appointments was occurring in the business-oriented disciplines, but Political Economy was getting quite different treatment. A charitable view would be that an accountant's mentality towards a discipline in financial deficit had replaced ideological antipathy as the main obstacle. However, the appearance of a deficit in Political Economy arose from the particular accounting practice employed. Disciplines were not simply funded according to the number of students they taught. Those with higher proportions of international fee-paying students were given higher financial allocations, even though the fee-paying students had generally been attracted to the Faculty rather than to individual disciplines. As one political economy student writing in *Honi Soit* pointed out, this financial model made a mockery of the claim that 'admitting fee-paying students directly benefits HECS students because their fees are used to improve teaching quality through their cross-subsidisation of HECS-centred programs'.[26] The model resulted in the relative impoverishment of the Discipline of Government and International Relations as well as Political Economy.

Beyond the accountant's mentality, a lack of empathy with the challenging and critical character of the subject matter of political economy may also be discerned. The dean's rhetoric commonly stressed synergies between social sciences and business studies, but the practice seemed somewhat different. Perhaps the inclination of some of the political economists towards occasional anti-capitalist sentiments was irksome. Individual political economy staff were, presumably, also irritants because of their known reservations about some of the Faculty policies. One, for example, talked to the press about the problems of maintaining educational quality in an era when fee revenues from international students with poor English language competence had become the paramount concern. The dean was known to be ropeable and felt it necessary to write to all Faculty alumni in an attempt to deny any slippage of educational standards.

The political economy staff had difficulty in coping with the fiscal austerity imposed on the discipline and their declining number. Parts of the political economy program, including the Master's course and units of study for honours students, had to be pared back because of resource shortages. The students were generally understanding, recognising the structural origins of the cuts, but staff morale became a significant problem. Some of the academics anticipated that further attrition would eventually result in the dean winding up the Discipline

---

[26] Jeffrey Wilson, 'Sorry Frank: Or how I learnt to stop worrying and love the fee-payers,' *Honi Soit*, Week 10, Semester 1, 2006.

of Political Economy, as had happened to the Discipline of Economic History. The possibility of amalgamating with another department was explored, but there were no takers. There was also talk among some of the political economy staff of trying to find jobs in other disciplines before the axe fell.

A small band of undergraduate student activists provided impetus for a more positive response. They included Kristie Flannery, Amanda McCormack, Isobelle Barrett Meyering, Jeremy Skellern, Jeffrey Wilson and others on the executive of the revitalised political economy students' society (ECOPSoc). Working in tandem with those political economy staff who had maintained a 'never say die' attitude, they became actively involved in lobbying for more resources. They emphasised the need for a change in the Faculty's funding model, and wrote articles for *Honi Soit* to publicise their concerns. A special feature of *Honi* was produced in June 2006, its editorial noting that it was exactly twenty-three years since *Honi* had produced a special PE issue in June 1983, 'when most of us hadn't even been born'.[27]

The political economy students also organised a demonstration, reviving the tradition of in-person student activism that had characterised earlier struggles for political economy. The demo focused on a Merewether Lecture Theatre where a faculty meeting was being held in May 2006. About two dozen students picketed the event, plastering the walls with posters and holding placards in support of political economy students' rights. Some of them moved, uninvited, into the meeting room and, after the dean had presented his usual lengthy report on faculty issues, they posed challenging questions to him about faculty funding and political economy students' interests. By comparison with student protests in the 1970s and 1980s, this was

---

[27] *Honi Soit*, Week 12, Semester 1, 2006.

Students take action to defend Political Economy

by **Isobelle Barrett Meyering and Jeff Wilson**

Political Economy students have begun their campaign to defend and improve conditions in the Department. In a letter sent to the Dean of Economics and Business last week, the Political Economy Society outlined a series of demands.

The Society called for the maintenance of Political Economy as a distinct

When asked at the meeting how funding would be distributed to departments under the new structure, the Dean, Professor Peter Wolnizer, responded: "My opinion and what will be the basis of the Faculty's funding structure, is the principle that monies ought to flow to disciplines on their basis of their taught load and the profile of that load".

While the Dean refused to give any further details regarding the funding structure, it was implied that departments with

has been won through struggle, and it is unfortunate that this continues to this day. But if struggle is what is required, students will stand in solidarity with staff."

The Political Economy Society meets on the Wentworth Lawns at 5pm Tuesdays, and always welcomes new members, both Political Economy students and others equally disturbed by what these changes mean for HECS students university-wide.

Figure 34. Article from *Honi Soit*, Week 10, Semester 1, 2006 (extract).

low-key protest activity. However, it did signal that the political economy student movement was capable of reinvigoration even in an era when students were generally regarded as quiescent.

Meanwhile, an escape route appeared with the prospect of political economy shifting to the Faculty of Arts. As noted in a preceding chapter, the possibility of a faculty reshuffle had been mooted by the Vice-Chancellor back in February 1984, but had come to nought at that time. Now, twenty-one years later, June Sinclair, a recently appointed Pro-Vice-Chancellor with responsibilities for both the Faculty of Economics and Business and for the Faculty of Arts, sought to shift the Discipline of Government and International Relations from the former faculty to the latter. Political Economy staff watched the process with interest, knowing that any such relocation would probably have ramifications for them too. Although a rearguard action by the academic staff in the Department of Government thwarted Sinclair's initiative, it became increasingly clear during this episode that the dean of the Faculty of Economics and Business did not see these two disciplines as central to his future plans. The question of whether political economy would have a better future in Arts began to be seriously considered.

The mechanism to make the faculty restructuring actually happen was devised in 2006 by Don Nutbeam, who held the newly-created position of provost, carrying the overall responsibility for the University's academic arrangements. Nutbeam established a committee to review the future of the social sciences at the university. The immediate antecedents of his action were, first, the publication in *The Australian* newspaper of an article by political economist Gavan Butler that decried the damage being done to teaching and research in the social sciences in the Faculty of Economics and Business, and, second, a meeting between Butler and the Vice-Chancellor, Gavin Brown, at which Butler suggested that the University might usefully initiate an inquiry into the most appropriate way to protect and develop the social sciences at Sydney.

Unlike earlier inquiries, the one set up by Nutbeam was not explicitly concerned with conflicts between mainstream and political economics. Rather, its focus was on a broader consideration of what restructuring of departments, schools and faculties might best serve the goal of improving teaching and research in the social sciences. Nutbeam invited Tom Kvan, dean of the Faculty of Architecture, to chair the small committee of inquiry. The committee invited submissions from interested parties, just as the previous committees of inquiry into political economy headed by Mills, Ward and Wilkes in the 1970s and 1980s had done. Several of the submissions were written by political economy staff, students and alumni, emphasising the importance of political economy within the social sciences.

Kvan's committee produced its report at the start of 2007, recommending that a new School of Social Inquiry should be created in the Faculty of Arts and that the disciplines of Political Economy and Government and International Relations be relocated to it, along with the existing Arts departments of Sociology and Social Policy, Anthropology and the Centre for Peace and Conflict Studies. It also recommended the establishment of an institute to coordinate research and teaching between a broader range of departments in other faculties with interests in social sciences. These recommendations were accepted by the provost and the University's Academic Board, although Nutbeam decided that the name of the new school should be changed to Social and Political Sciences to accommodate the preference of the staff in Government and International Relations.

So from January 2008 onwards, Political Economy became a department in the Faculty of Arts. The staff did not have to physically move right away: they stayed in their existing offices for the time being and most of the political economy classes continued to be held in and around Merewether. Much else changed though. For the first time the two rival groups of economists were in different faculties and accountable to different deans and heads of schools.

Degrees had to be restructured. In the first instance, the degrees in which political economy had been typically studied—the Bachelor of Economic and Social Sciences and the Bachelor of International Studies—would also become Faculty of Arts degrees; and committees were set up to amalgamate them with two existing Arts degrees called Bachelor of Social Sciences and Bachelor of Global Studies. These committees, comprising staff from the five departments in the new School of Social and Political Sciences, reported in early 2008, recommending that the Economic and Social Sciences degree be retained for the following year, with political economy as a core component, but that from 2009 onward the International Studies and

Global Studies degrees should be merged into a new degree, to be called International and Global Studies. The latter change removed the core status that political economy had previously had in the degree but gave it a smaller role within new interdisciplinary units that all students would be required to study. Political economist Dick Bryan was invited by the dean to be the director of studies for the newly merged degree, while Frank Stilwell continued to act as director of the Bachelor of Economic and Social Sciences during the period of transition.

These changes to faculty arrangements and degree structures were not driven directly by the interests of the political economy staff and students. Indeed, unlike the reforms arising from the committees chaired by Mills, Ward and Wilkes, the Kvan committee's report did not explicitly address the political economy dispute. Political economy was explicitly mentioned in only two sentences, which said:

> To achieve academic coherence, intellectual scale and viability ... the school must include social science disciplines outside the Faculty of Arts, in particular those of Political Science and Political Economy ... [The] establishment of a School of Social Inquiry without either political science or political economy would be a meaningless gesture.

Concern not to reignite the dispute may have been a consideration in the minds of at least some university administrators, but more general pull and push factors were evidently operating. A pull factor was the wish of the Faculty of Arts—which the *Times Higher Educational Supplement* had recently ranked fifth in the world for the humanities—to strengthen its teaching and research in social sciences. A push factor was the drive by those with power in the Faculty of Economics and Business to remove those subject areas that did not fit the preferred professional business school model.

That the dean of the Faculty of Economics and Business was relaxed about waving farewell to the political economists is in little doubt, notwithstanding his periodic speeches about the value of social sciences in his faculty. The written response he made to the official social sciences review, supposedly on behalf of the Faculty (but never put to, nor endorsed by, a faculty meeting), did not argue the case for retaining Political Economy and Government and International Relations as disciplines in the Faculty. Indeed, neither subject area was mentioned at all, so it was reasonable to infer that they were not wanted. It was also reasonable to infer that a mixture of ideological and financial considerations mingled in arriving at that judgement. In other words, the Faculty of Economics and Business, as a centre for business and management education, would be better off if it dispensed with disciplines that might be conducive to understanding the contemporary business environment[28] but which, at the bottom line, did not contribute directly to its profits.

Most of the political economy staff thought that joining the new School of Social and Political Sciences in the Faculty of Arts would be a positive step. Eventually, all decided to embrace the change, recognising that, at the very least, it would be a better option than staying in a faculty where they were not valued and were being starved of resources. More positively, they recognised that the change opened up possibilities for closer ties with cognate social sciences, thereby providing the basis for an improved environment for interdisciplinary research, teaching and learning. In the first year in their new school, the political economists developed cross-listings for new units of study with sociology, anthropology and peace and conflict studies.

---

[28] It is pertinent to note that it was the Department of Political Economy, not the Department of Economics nor any other part of the Faculty of Economics and Business, that put on a university-wide symposium to consider the nature of the emerging global financial crisis as it was developing in October 2008.

What of student opinions? Unlike at other phases in the history of the political economy struggle, these played little direct role in the faculty reorganisation process of 2007. Indeed, as the political economy students came to be aware of the changes being proposed, their typical complaint was that there had been inadequate consultation and regard for their own interests, such as in maintaining the existing arrangements for the successful Bachelor of International Studies and Bachelor of Economic and Social Sciences degrees. This time there were no major demonstrations on the campus, however, but there was significant student involvement of a less dramatic form. Several articles in *Honi Soit* emphasised the uncertainty that had been created for political economy students about what courses would be available to them in the future. The executive members of ECOPSoc also made submissions to the committee of inquiry into the future of the social sciences and made personal representation to the dean of Faculty of Economics and Business, in which they stressed the importance of maintaining studies in political economy. These were constructive engagements, showing careful judgements about the most effective interventions in university decision-making processes.

The new Political Economy Alumni Society also played an active role. Its formation in 2006 had been largely driven by concerns among recent graduates—such as Darren Rodrigo, Anna Samson, Chris Jefferis and Ben Spies Butcher—about the threats to the future of the political economy program. Former University of Sydney political economy student Greg Combet (then ACTU president and later to become a member of federal parliament) flew from Melbourne to address the inaugural meeting in the Wentworth Building in November 2006. The activists who formed the Alumni Society had already made significant interventions into the faculty restructuring process, sending a deputation to the dean of the Faculty of Economics and Business and putting a submission to the social sciences review. The tradition of students and staff working together to defend and extend the political economy program was being expanded to include former students. Without that initiative it would have been easier for the University to terminate the political economy program—had it wanted to—and to disperse its remaining staff to other departments, as had happened with the Discipline of Economic History. Solidarity between student activists, alumni and staff saved the day.

By the time the Department of Political Economy was formally established within the School of Social and Political Sciences in the Faculty of Arts on 1 January 2008, over 12,000 students had been enrolled in one or more of the units of study in political economy. The primary goals articulated by the political economy movement in the 1970s—a full program of political economy courses and a separate department of political economy—had been attained. The shift to the new school also had expanded opportunities for the political economists to work cooperatively with social scientists from other departments in teaching and research. It is a context in which the Department of Political Economy can look forward to further developing its role in providing an alternative, progressive education.

Still pushing for political economy: Amanda McCormack

Political economy undergraduate student, 2004–8, and former president of the Political Economy Students' Society

Questioning and showing the flaws in the dominant discourses of society, especially those discourses used as foundations for social policy, is always difficult. It takes huge energy and commitment to continue when met with disdain and hostility. Yet students are still fighting to ensure that political economy, as a dissident discipline, exists at Sydney University. The social context in which we find ourselves today is quite different from the radicalism that was very apparent in the 1970s. Even so, students are still willing to commit to ensuring the longevity of political economy as an academic discipline with the same passion and commitment.

The three years from 2004 to 2007 in particular were very difficult for political economy, which was starved of funds because it did not bring in enough full fee-paying students (international or domestic). It also faced a faculty leadership that did not seem to understand its importance in the curriculum and retiring political economy staff were not replaced. So students once again decided to fight to ensure that political economy survived.

Through the Political Economy Society (affectionately known as ECOPSoc), students rallied during 2006 and 2007. While the actions we took were a little different to those of our 1970s counterparts, and our numbers were fewer, we managed to be quite effective. What wound up happening was in part intended to quell the prospect of more student dissent.

Our campaign to secure a firmer future for political economy studies was largely about engaging with the managerialism that currently permeates the university, which affects how decisions are made. It was about understanding the details of faculty funding models and articulating our objections to the inequality that arose from the ways that disciplines within the faculty were resourced. It was also about engaging with the university bureaucracy, about writing submissions, explaining to other students what was going on and seeking to get them involved. As a result of our education in political economy, we were able to understand, engage and convey clearly within the academic community what we wanted, which surprised the faculty administration in an era when they expected students to be more passive, more accepting of what was placed before them.

We also rallied and had the colour and movement that is necessary for any campaign. We painted banners, printed T-shirts, prepared and distributed leaflets. On one occasion, in 2006, we greeted faculty board members as they arrived at their meeting by forming a double line of students to present them with our letter of demand, as well as decorating the walls and desks of the faculty board meeting room with that letter. We liaised with other faculty student clubs about how we were being affected by the faculty funding model, and put together a special edition of *Honi Soit* on the continuing struggle for political economy. These are the activities that are always the most fun of any campaign.

Given that the Faculty of Economics and Business had not had that level of student interest in a while, we were certainly noticed. And, as it turned out, the faculty eventually decided to change the way in which disciplines were funded towards a method that was fairer and, surprisingly, that addressed the concerns that were initially raised at our meeting with the dean. Despite political economy moving out of that faculty at the start of 2008, ECOPSoc helped to ensure that other disciplines would not be deleteriously affected by a funding model that discriminates against those who do not bring in a lot of external funding.

To keep the momentum of the campaign going, we wanted to ensure that we had representation on the faculty boards for Economics and Business, and for Arts—which we achieved. In 2006, the election of the undergraduate student representative to the Economics and Business Faculty Board was hotly contested; of three positions available, two of our candidates managed to get elected. Our third candidate missed out, but only just: she tied third and hers was not the name that was pulled out of the hat.

At the same time as the machinations of the faculty were going on, a university review of the social sciences was announced. Because political economy was specifically named in the review, we wanted to be involved, and to make sure we were heard. At the public briefings, we reported back what was going on. We wrote submissions, met with the Social Sciences Review reference group and presented students' concerns. The recommended repositioning of political economy into the Faculty of Arts is an outcome that could provide a more secure future for the discipline. ECOPSoc still takes an interest in what is going on and keeps its finger on the pulse.

On reflection, this campaign has been the most fun of my university life so far. When I moved half way across the country to study at Sydney University, I had no idea that this kind of experience was possible, or that I would be joining with my fellow students to ensure that political economy would continue to be taught. When I hear about the political campaigns of the 1970s, I see parallels with what we did and will continue to do, despite a rather different context. Most importantly, the campaign illustrated that students can affect change within a currently managerialist and changing academy, especially when we work together.

7
What's wrong with economics?

An analysis of any dispute requires delving below its surface manifestations—as described in the preceding six chapters—to see the underlying sources of tension. In the political economy dispute the nature of economics as a discipline is one obvious source. Attitudes to the processes of teaching and learning are another. A third concerns the power structures within which decisions are made. In pursuit of a deeper understanding of what has been at stake, this chapter and the next examine these interrelated sources of tension.

The most fundamental element in the conflict has been the nature of the subject matter of economics. Most academic economists have a strong attachment to a particular body of theory and it is this that the political economists have consistently sought to challenge. At the core of mainstream economics is neoclassical theory, which had its origins around the 1870s, after which economics developed into a specialised discipline. The issues of politics, history and social structure that had been integral to the concerns of the earlier classical political economists were, and still are, largely unaddressed by that theory.

The core of the neoclassical paradigm consists of a body of assumptions and a set of propositions that follow, in principle, as logical deductions from those assumptions. Key assumptions are:

- the primacy of the individual as the basic unit of analysis
- the view of the individual as a rational calculating machine in pursuit of maximum material gain

- an assumed decision-making environment that comprises an economic sphere in which many independent agents interact in all-pervasive competitive markets (which, in the extreme, eradicate individual discretion), and a political sphere containing a government whose principal role is to support the appropriate economic environment
- an assumption of sufficient information to make (individual) rational calculation possible, preferably either full information or probabilistic uncertainty
- the view that the price mechanism tends to act to stabilise the economy as a whole.

The vision of an economy that is atomistic yet stable was originally borrowed from classical mechanics. 'Physics envy' is a tongue-in-cheek term favoured by some critics of neoclassical economics.[29] If economic behaviour is represented as a mechanical process, understanding it is a matter of logic. In the aggregate, economic behaviour is structurally constrained by market-dictated prices, and it has its own inbuilt mechanisms to re-establish stability following disturbances.

This structure constitutes a particular concept of social order. Represented under the label 'general equilibrium', it takes an essentially mechanical form because relevant behaviour is dictated by an omnipresent and ruthlessly efficient resource allocation mechanism embodied in the impersonal, competitive price system. The theory is formally modelled by using mathematical techniques borrowed from other disciplines (in particular, calculus and linear algebra).

---

[29] This phrase is used by Brian Toohey in his book *Tumbling dice: the story of modern economic policy*, Heinemann, Melbourne, 1994, p. 57.

Based on these principles, conventional economic analysis has been developed, at its best, into an extraordinarily elegant edifice but one that is, at its worst, spectacularly out of touch with reality. This edifice serves two functions in which form and content are brilliantly fused: an analytical one in which an elegance of form is pursued for its own sake, and an ideological one in which all the contradictions of liberal social philosophy are resolved in the *deus ex machina* of an atomistic self-regulating market economy. Therein lies the underpinning of economic rationalism or, more generally, the neoliberal economic perspective that has been so influential in recent decades. Of course, not all economists subscribe to the value judgements associated with neoliberalism, and much work of an empirical nature takes place within the economics discipline; but the conceptual home base of mainstream economics continues to be the core neoclassical theory. Moreover, the status hierarchy of academic economists within the discipline is directly related to the proximity of their research work to that theory. The more theoretically refined the analysis, the higher the disciplinary status.

It was this neoclassical economics on which the syllabus preferred by the professors of economics at the University of Sydney from 1969 onwards was based, and it was the dominant position of neoclassical economics within the core undergraduate courses to which the dissidents were opposed.[30] In this respect, the conflict at the University of Sydney has mirrored a broader and more long-standing conflict in the economics profession, nationally and internationally.

---

[30] An early critique of orthodox economics was originally presented in draft form by sacked tutor Bill Waters at the Radical Economics conference in 1973. It was subsequently co-authored with Ted Wheelwright and published as 'University economics: a radical critique' in *The Australian Quarterly*, vol. 45, no. 3, September 1973, pp. 51–65 and subsequently in E.L.Wheelwright & F. Stilwell (eds), *Readings in political economy*, vol. 1, ANZ Book Co., Sydney, 1976.

Over the twentieth century, there was a persistent confrontation between the rigidity of this neoclassical analytical structure and the analytical requirements of studying complex historical processes and institutional behaviour. In practice, this confrontation produced, not a modification of the neoclassical analysis, but a stronger commitment to an increasingly refined version. The different analytical approach of classical and Marxist economics was seldom acknowledged, other than as an illustration of discredited pre-neoclassical views. A more pragmatic institutional economics flourished, particularly in the USA, during the first half of the twentieth century, although it was largely purged from mainstream economics textbooks after the Second World War. It has only recently been deemed to be acceptable in a revised form as 'new institutionalism' to the extent that it has embraced the methodological individualism of neoclassical theory.

The principal conceptual breakaway to have been institutionally successful (accepted in the compulsory economics syllabus and as a basis for respectable research) was Keynesian macroeconomics. This has provided an alternative vision of the economy at the aggregate level, and is not integrally dependent upon individualist analysis. John Maynard Keynes understood neoclassical theory but saw it as incapable of explaining, still less of resolving, the problems of unemployment and economic stability experienced by capitalism in practice. His major intellectual (and ideological) contribution was the view that free market capitalism has an innate flaw: the lack of an automatic mechanism to guarantee the stable full employment of resources. Keynesianism was introduced into the conventional syllabus throughout English-language countries in the 1950s and 1960s. (University of Sydney political economist Geelum Simpson-Lee's textbook for HSC students, written in conjunction with Cyril Renwick, was one vehicle for this in Australia.) But combining some aspects of Keynesian economics with neoclassical theory (the so-called neoclassical synthesis) reduced the former's role to a subsidiary one of generating recommendations for quite narrowly conceived economic policy (macroeconomic fine tuning) while competitive markets—and the supposed theoretical integrity of the neoclassical system—remained intact. Indeed, the neoclassical synthesis contrived in the USA attested that Keynes' *General Theory* was really just a special case of the more general neoclassical theory.

The remnants of Keynesianism (and its progressive ideological implications) came under escalating attack from the 1970s onwards, with the ascendancy of a more orthodox macroeconomics. The monetarists, led by free-market guru Milton Friedman, took the view that money markets are well behaved and capable of adjusting savings, private investment and consumption; thus, not only is central bank manipulation of money markets unnecessary, but it is also dysfunctional. Monetarism saw the problems that beset the economy (such as economic cycles and inflation) as the effect of the excessive variations by central banks in the money supply. This shifted the blame from the private sector and the instability of profit expectations onto 'external' factors such as government incompetence and irresponsibility. Monetarism shared with neoclassicism a common ideological preference for a market economy free of (unwarranted) government intervention. The running debate between self-styled Keynesians and monetarists, which peaked in the 1970s and 1980s, created the impression of disciplinary diversity, but it defined the limits of acceptable debate. It paved the way for the ascendancy of 'new classical macroeconomics' in the 1990s, essentially a reassertion of pre-Keynesian beliefs purporting to show that the economy works best when governments interfere least.

Subsequent currents in the economic mainstream have incorporated a variety of other ideas, including rational expectations theory, new growth theories, behavioural economics and game theory. Game theory, for example, is regarded by some economists as providing new conceptual foundations, although it has difficulty producing the unambiguous results to which economists seeking a scientific status for their discipline aspire. It provides a partial challenge to the general equilibrium tradition in economic theory, just as behavioural economics questions the assumption of instrumental rationality underpinning the notion of 'rational economic man'. Game theory now has a significant place in the graduate microeconomics syllabus. In the teaching of core undergraduate economics, however, the neoclassical approach remains hegemonic.

The critics of the dominant paradigm have been many, varied and persistent.[31] Dissident economists have argued that neoclassical theory, with or without these contemporary add-ons and variations, is incapable in practice of illuminating the evolutionary character and power relationships within capitalist economies. They have articulated alternative understandings that have continued to grow in sophistication; but mainstream economics sails on regardless.

---

[31] See, for example, B. Ward, *What's wrong with economics?*, Macmillan, London, 1972; M. Hollis and E.J. Nell, *Rational economic man: a philosophical critique of neoclassical economics*, Cambridge University Press, Cambridge, 1975; L. Thurow, *Dangerous currents: the state of economics*, Oxford University Press, Oxford, 1983; P. Ormerod, *The death of economics*, Faber and Faber, London, 1994; E. Jones, 'The tyranny of a priorism in economic thought,' *History of Economics Review*, no. 22, Summer 1994; R. Heilbroner & W. Milberg, *The crisis of vision in modern economic thought*, Cambridge University Press, Cambridge, 1995; S. Keen, *Debunking economics: the naked emperor of the social sciences*, Pluto Press Australia, Sydney, 2001; E. Fullbrook (ed), *The crisis in economics*, Routledge, London, 2003; F. Ackerman & A. Nadal, *The flawed foundations of general equilibrium: critical essays in economic theory*, Routledge, New York, 2004; S. Marglin, *The dismal science: how thinking like an economist undermines community*, Harvard University Press, Cambridge, 2008; and E. Fullbrook (ed), *Pluralist economics*, Zed Books, London, 2009.

There is a particular curiosum that needs to be noted at this point. It concerns the emergence over the past few decades of a political economy of the right. This thrust has been embodied in disparate developments: an economic history school (led by Douglass North), an economic theory of politics and public choice theory (pioneered by James Buchanan and others), a 'new institutionalism' (building on the work of Ronald Coase) and a defence of the large corporation as the centrepiece of competition (the Chicago school). Curiously, at no time did any variant of right-wing political economy, including the long-standing Austrian school, receive more than a passing nod from the leadership of the Department of Economics at the University of Sydney (while the political economy of the right did receive some attention in the political economy program). In various North American universities such political economy, alongside neoclassical orthodoxy, is a notable feature of the curriculum. The point is of some significance in illustrating that political economy is not inherently associated with the political left, and that it depends on how the term is used. Implicitly or explicitly, all economics is political.

The *explicitly* political application of neoclassical economic theory is evident in so-called economic rationalism. As the core of mainstream economics was purged of the influence of Keynesianism and refocused on a more purist neoclassical theory, it is remarkable that the orthodoxy came, during the last quarter of the twentieth century, to be more influential in the realm of public policy.[32] This economic rationalist approach to economic policy, underpinning neoliberalism more generally, prioritises private sector control of the economy as a

---

[32] A controversial work emphasising the influence of mainstream economics on public policy in Australia was M. Pusey, *Economic rationalism in Canberra: a nation-building state changes its mind*, Cambridge University Press, Cambridge, 1991; on economic rationalism see also the earlier study by F. Stilwell, 'Economic Rationalism is Irrational,' *Arena*, no. 87, 1989, pp. 139–46.

matter of principle. The rhetoric is associated with the advocacy of privatisation, deregulation and the liberalisation of trade and investment, although in practice these processes have been selectively applied for the benefit of particular private interests. Some neoclassical economists see this economic rationalism in public policy as a vulgar application—even violation—of their more sophisticated theories. However, the practical test of an idea is its real-world influence. By that criterion few would doubt that neoclassical economics has provided a particularly influential way of seeing (and way of changing) the world in which we live. It is little exaggeration to say that the proponents of orthodoxy have sought to reconstruct the real world in the image of a neoclassical world.

Meanwhile, many mainstream economists have continued to assert the 'value free' nature of their discipline in their undergraduate teaching and textbooks, if not in their personal practice. It is an assertion that the political economists at the University of Sydney focused particularly on discrediting, arguing that economic analyses have always been used for political purposes and to support particular sectional or class interests. Political economists have also emphasised that the core of the economics discipline is substantially inadequate as an explanatory device. The commitment to a highly restrictive method (one of logical determinism) and a particular vision (a pervasive and all-powerful market mechanism) produces an analysis ill-suited to explaining actual economic systems, characterised by institutions with varying degrees of power interacting in a complex and often contradictory manner, and subject to perennial challenges and crises.

The conventional paradigm has served to support the political economic *status quo*. It mainly does so not by explicit support but by obfuscation. The defence of the *status quo* involves an incoherent mixture of a reification of an ideal market economy with a pragmatic acknowledgement of some contemporary institutional realities, overlaid with an unarticulated class prejudice. Union power is represented as an impediment to a mythical free labour market. Corporate market power, while also being derogated in principle, tends to be accepted as a possible solution to some market coordination problems. Government involvement, which has always been integral to the capitalist economy, is labelled as 'intervention', its impact is criticised as 'distorting' and it is perennially suspect because it creates 'rents'. Examples of alleged government failure are so continuously adduced as to deflect attention from the inadequacies of outcomes derived from economic relations between private agents of greatly different power (a tiny number of pharmaceutical companies facing inadequately informed medical practitioners, myriad small-scale drug dispensaries and millions of unorganised sick people, for example).

At the macroeconomic level there is visceral support of wage reduction through political means in the interests of healthy profit levels and viable economic growth. This imperative, so-called, is disconnected from respectable theories of national income distribution in which wage and profit shares are dictated by the objective contributions of labour and capital to production. The examples could be multiplied. In general, the effect of a convoluted combination of abstract theory, pragmatism and prejudice is to support the interests of capital against labour and consumers, and the interests of more powerful sections of business against smaller businesses; but the support is neither intellectually coherent nor morally explicit.

Political economy stands in contrast to neoclassical theory essentially because of its evolutionary perspective rather than a focus on equilibrium conditions. Political economists have sought to examine and develop alternative explanations of contemporary capitalism, and to illuminate the character of socioeconomic change and the forces generating such change. Together these explanations constitute what Professor Joan Robinson called 'non-neoclassical economics', and others more recently have called 'heterodox economics'.[33] The alternatives have shared a focus on the historical development and contemporary behaviour of key institutions and their structure, and thus a concern for both agency and structure. Variously, the alternatives to neoclassicism have been preoccupied with subsets of institutions (such as associations between businesses, the state apparatus, the organisation of labour, the family and gender relations, and so on). At the same time political economists have acknowledged the force of the imperatives of a production system that is fundamentally capitalist. Economic and social order exists, despite the complexity of influences operating within an economic system, but it is not the simple product of demand-supply interactions in the market. Thus political economists focus on the regulatory institutions, conceivably more powerful than the market, that are the products of purposeful human agency and designed to achieve outcomes that the market cannot achieve.

All strands of political economic analysis, drawing on the conceptual frameworks of Marxism, institutional economics, post-Keynesian economics, feminist and environmental studies, have used a method that has been historically based and empirically grounded. Moreover, all strands recognise that useful social science analysis must cross received disciplinary boundaries and that other disciplines have also brought important insights to bear on understanding economic and social order and development.

---

[33] An indication of the range of alternative approaches to non-neoclassical economics can be seen in the special issue of the *Journal of Australian Political Economy* on 'The state of political economy,' no. 50, December 2002.

These are the principles that informed the construction of the political economy courses at the University of Sydney from the start—the need to explore competing schools of economic thought as well as the neoclassical paradigm, the recognition of methodological pluralism, the need to study historical processes and to take an interdisciplinary approach that situates economic enquiry in the broader context of the social sciences.

None of these concerns about economics and political economy is specific to the University of Sydney. This particular university has been unusual, however, because of its local concentration of dissident voices. Political economists exist in departments of other universities but typically have lacked the critical mass to mount an effective challenge to the orthodoxy. Ted Wheelwright had been in that position at the University of Sydney during the 1950s and 1960s, as a relatively lone voice promoting the ideas of dissident economists outside the mainstream (such as Marx, Veblen, Hilferding and Hobson) and doing empirical research into controversial contemporary concerns (such as the impact of foreign ownership on the development of Australian manufacturing industry). It was only when Wheelwright (along with some increasingly disenchanted colleagues) was joined in the early 1970s by other dissenting economists—all with mainstream training but starting to explore alternatives to neoclassical economics—that a critical mass capable of becoming a potent force for challenge and change was established.[34]

---

[34] During the peak of the dispute at the University of Sydney intellectual exchange between the mainstream economists and political economists was less common than were confrontations over decision-making. An exception was during 1975 when papers written by staff about on methodology in economics were circulated, presented and discussed at two seminars. Colin Simkin's paper restated Karl Popper's views on method; the critique by Evan Jones was more akin to Thomas Kuhn's, with its emphasis on paradigms and paradigmatic shifts. Debesh

In this process of challenge and change, the focus on the nature of economics as a discipline was fused with considerations about how it should be taught and how such educational policy decisions should be made.

Relaxing the economic assumptions: Marian Baird

Political economy student activist in the 1970s; now Associate Professor in Work and Organisational Studies at the University of Sydney

In 1974 I enrolled in an economics degree at the University of Sydney. I was just seventeen, just out of an all-girls' Catholic high school on Sydney's northern beaches and very eager to expand my academic and political horizons. The Whitlam era had begun and my father's endorsement for university students rang in my ears—'Go out and demonstrate'. Within the year that's exactly what I was doing, along with many other Sydney Uni students. For the next few years we lived, breathed, ate, partied and travelled through political economy—PE. We fought the University and the establishment for course recognition, staff tenure and staff promotion. We fought and—mostly—won.

Three decades later, I can remember those days vividly and exactly. As I had less direct connections with the staff, most of my experiences were the result of student interaction and involvement. I love to recall the richness of those university days: the fun, the feelings, the drama and the tensions of the PE movement. I know now, even if I wasn't fully aware then, that political economy changed and enriched my life, and influenced how I now see the world in all my roles—woman, citizen, parent and academic. Even though my academic career took a slightly different direction, it remains grounded in my PE days. I still get a shimmer of excitement when students tell me they are studying PE.

Bhattacharya, Frank Stilwell and Gavan Butler also circulated papers, emphasising the interactions of methodology, ideology and pedagogy.

What attracted me to political economy and the political economy movement? It was a mixture of ideas and people. 'Let's assume ...' was the constant refrain of the economics course I studied. Why did we have to assume everything away, when clearly what we were assuming away was the very stuff of economic life? Without a doubt I was theoretically naïve, yet it made obvious and absolute sense to me that political economy provided far better explanations than neoclassical economics for understanding the domestic and international economy.

As well as being much more interesting academically, PE was far more personally challenging. The students and staff I met through PE opened my eyes to new ways of thinking and challenged all of my beliefs, everything a good university education should do. We were privileged and lucky: we had no tuition fees to pay and little need or enthusiasm for excessive consumption. Indian skirts and cheesecloth tops, no cars or mobile phones, run-down houses and cheap Newtown rents meant that we spent a lot of time in and around Uni, often sitting on the lawn outside Merewether with other PE activists, talking and debating student politics, religion, ethics and morals endlessly; we never discussed fashion, food or phones. At PE meetings I was inspired by the student leaders and confronted by some of the more outspoken PE women to think about feminism. I spoke out in lectures and demanded that fellow students in geography and industrial relations rally with the PE crowd.

There was the thrill and trepidation of the demonstrations, the mobilisation of students, wearing PE T-shirts and carrying PE banners, who marched from Merewether to the Front Lawn, and then occupied the Vice-Chancellor's office. I'll never forget the sound of the loudspeaker and the chant: 'What do we want? Political Economy. When do we want it? Now!' These demonstrations took a lot of preparation. We spent hours in the Tin Sheds designing and screen printing posters and nights traversing the University grounds, avoiding the 'grey men' from security while we plastered the campus with the results of our screen printing.

In 1975 I enrolled in the political economy conversion course, the course we won for students to transfer out of economics over to PE. What I learnt in that course and in subsequent PE studies, as well as my experiences as a student in the political economy movement at the University of Sydney in the 1970s, shaped me as a person. I'll never forget: 'Dare to struggle, dare to win.'

What's wrong with economics? • 117

Figure 35. Political economy poster from the 1970s: a theme still relevant to education today?

8
Pedagogy and power

Disagreement among the economists at the University of Sydney and elsewhere has not been limited to differing perceptions of the discipline and appropriate directions for its development, as discussed in the preceding chapter. Also important—some would say even more important—are differences in attitudes to teaching and learning. These attitudes were crucial in the early stages of the political economy dispute. Indeed, student unrest over the quality of undergraduate teaching pre-dated concerns about the biased content of the curriculum itself. In the late-1960s and early-1970s lectures in Economics I and (the macroeconomics part of) Economics II were notoriously badly presented, with students having difficulty taking clear notes, let alone deriving any insight into how the economy of the real world operated. This concern subsequently came to be linked to conflicts over curriculum design.

From the early 1970s onwards, the dissident staff group within the Department of Economics took the view that students should have the opportunity to explore the major competing schools of economic thought during their first year of studies and then specialise in political economy or mainstream economics thereafter. Other academic staff (some of whom, such as Peter Groenewegen, declared an interest in political economy) held that a conventional syllabus structure dominated by mainstream economics was appropriate for undergraduate students: that is, that they should study mainstream economics first and alternative currents of political economy (maybe) later.

The different attitudes to teaching involved—and continue to involve—more than matters of lecture and tutorial content. Essentially, the dissident students and the staff members of the Political Economy Group reacted against what they interpreted as authoritarian professorial attitudes and practices: the refusal to institutionalise student course questionnaires and learn from student feedback, a callous attitude towards high failure rates, the overreliance on conventional examinations in aggregate assessment and a reluctance to permit undergraduates to undertake independent self-generated projects and theses. All of these concerns became explicit at one time or another. And there were others. The question of student opinion, for example, was of particular importance in the context of the political economy dispute. Systematic student evaluations of courses were unusual in the 1970s and the University of Sydney was slow in institutionalising them. The repudiation of students' views by the professors of economics on such occasions when course questionnaires *were* conducted had damaging effects on student morale and was a significant spur to dissident students and staff.

Of course, conflict on issues of curriculum, teaching quality and assessment has been fairly standard fare in many university courses. What appears rather distinctive (albeit not unique) about mainstream economics is that, given the lack of an obvious association between much of the curriculum content and the observable character of the real world, an authoritarian teaching practice becomes normal, if not essential. The right to define the discipline is monopolised by the authorities, the result of which is that official student feedback is either minimised or deflected. This tendency came to be particularly well developed in the Department of Economics at the University of Sydney. Indeed, it was the standard of teaching of the compulsory courses by those of professorial rank and their denial of the legitimacy of adverse student opinion that initially fuelled the rebellion by students.

Here, too, the role of a critical mass of dissenting (or merely open-minded) academic staff is important. There was, in the Department of Economics, an atypically large proportion of academics who were willing to question, and eventually reject, substantial parts of their formal education, to rebel against an illiberal hierarchy and to explore how different methods of teaching could develop student interest and produce a more enlightened education. Of course, teaching competence transcends affiliation with any political faction. Some of the lecturing staff who maintained allegiance to the prevailing professorial regime and the mainstream economics curriculum were individually committed to high educational standards. However, the dissident political economists set out to make a systematic *collective* effort at a sympathetic teaching practice.

Grand aims are not always consistently achieved. Other institutional pressures intervene. Staff have to find time for research as well as teaching. Resource shortages produce excessive tutorial class sizes, in political economy as elsewhere. The teaching standards of the political economy staff did not always live up to the collective ideal. And not all political economy students have been committed to high educational outcomes. However, the general experience has been of an unusual amount of intellectual excitement and exchange, manifest partly in the students' assertiveness and intellectual independence both in and out of the classroom. This situation contrasts with the tendency for the conventional economics syllabus to emphasise absorbing the set theories without the development of systematically critical thinking. According to regular questionnaires, student evaluation of the political economy courses has been generally positive.

Since university policy in the 1990s began to require such surveys in all units of study, political economy has shown consistently better outcomes than the units of study in mainstream economics. Statistics compiled in the Faculty of Economics and Business for 2003-7 showed that the mainstream economics courses, especially the first year undergraduate units, were typically the most lowly rated in the faculty while political economy courses were the highest rated.[35] Units of study taught in the Discipline of Government and International Relations typically rated highly too. Shifting these two disciplines to the Faculty of Arts in 2008 depleted the Faculty of Economics and Business of its two best performing teaching areas.

Can renewed dissent over the teaching of economics be anticipated? As opposed to what was available from the mid-1970s, when the political economy courses were introduced at the University of Sydney, most students in the Faculty of Economics and Business now have a limited choice. Units of study in mainstream economics are compulsory for undergraduate students in the commerce degree, although less in number than for the economics degree (in order not to 'crowd out' the space for taking lots of units of study in business subjects). Although those commerce degree students are denied a choice between mainstream economics and political economy, some have been able to take the latter in addition to the compulsory mainstream units. Since the 1990s students taking mainstream economics seem to have become increasingly compliant, perhaps because they regard an economics education, however restricted in vision, as a means to an end, such as employment in the finance sector.

One may also conjecture that, with the ascendancy of neoliberalism as the dominant political ideology in the last three decades, some students may have seen a more direct connection between neoclassical theory and contemporary economic policy. Indeed, 'free market economics' has developed a strongly prescriptive character,

---

[35] Evidence to support this claim is in the internal document produced by the Faculty of Economics and Business, 'Unit of Study Evaluations 2003–7'.

notwithstanding its deficiencies as a descriptive tool. By the same token, the case for an educational practice that encourages critical reflection on how economic theory is used and abused becomes correspondingly stronger. With the global financial crisis that began in 2008 being widely interpreted as a crisis of neoliberalism and financialisation, the orthodoxy's lack of credibility and durable value has again been thrown into stark relief. Whether this creates a milieu conducive to the resurgence of student dissent is uncertain. The substantive issues concerning the relevance and usefulness of a conventional economics education remain, although a more quiescent mood currently prevails.

What of the processes by which decisions are made about economics courses and other programs of study within the universities? A third element in the political economy dispute at the University of Sydney, combining with the concerns about subject matter and teaching, has been the institutional decision-making arrangements. 'Who has the power?' and 'How is it used?' are the central questions here. The political economy dispute brought them into sharp focus. It was the challenge mounted by the political economists and others to the prevailing university power structures that was for many—economists and non-economists—the most confronting aspect of the dispute.

Like most other universities, the University of Sydney has had a strongly hierarchical administrative structure. Dominant power has been traditionally vested in the Vice-Chancellor and academics of professorial rank (previously only people holding established chairs). Historically, the University's by-laws granted those of professorial rank monopoly rights in the definition of the nature of their disciplines and in the direction of teaching. In effect, these by-laws operated like an academic Masters and Servants Act, with heads of departments and other academic units being chosen by the Vice-Chancellor rather than being elected. The academic freedom of all

Figure 36. 1975 political economy poster emphasising the conflict with institutions within University hierarchy (design by Rod O'Donnell).

individual members of staff has always been an important, cherished feature of universities, of course; but decisions about educational structure, courses and resources have reflected a hierarchy of authority. There was some significant democratisation of administrative structures in the 1970s; yet, by the 1990s, a 'top-down' managerial variant of the old god-professor model had come to dominate, a process particularly evident in the Faculty of Economics.

When the political economy dispute was developing in the early 1970s, the tension between the 'top-down' power structure and the demands for participatory democracy was intense. From a staff perspective, a major complaint was that academics below the rank of full professor had almost no formal rights at the departmental level. The only significant exception was a subsection of the University by-laws that formally compelled a department head to convey to a faculty meeting any proposal supported by a majority of staff who were members of the faculty. This very limited recognition of the lecturing staff's intellectual capacity and rights made little difference in practice in the Department of Economics during the 1970s and 1980s, as the majority of the staff did not usually support course proposals that were made by the political economists and opposed by the professors. One can only speculate about the reasons for this, but support for the professors' general intellectual position, personal antipathy to the political economists, respect for authority *per se*, fear, careerism and desire for a quiet life all presumably played their parts. Such are the usual underpinnings of institutional conformity.

A strong hierarchy in constitutional terms was reinforced in the Department of Economics by the personal actions of Professors Hogan and Simkin and later by Professors Mills and Groenewegen. Some other departments continued to work reasonably well in the 1970s and 1980s because the professoriate did not seek to deny effective decision-making influence to the non-professorial staff. By contrast, the professors of economics interpreted their powers in the strictest sense, ensuring that the University's by-laws would be a living document. Student representation at the department level was generally denied throughout the period when the political economy dispute was at its height, although small numbers of students were allowed to attend and present proposals at departmental meetings on a few occasions and there were periodic staff-student consultative meetings, with no decision-making powers. In practice the token student representation that was formally introduced across the University in the 1980s made little ongoing difference, in spite of the calibre and commitment of many student representatives who put themselves forward. Typically, the academic staff did little to encourage active student participation and, by the 1990s, most student representation at the department level had disappeared. Again, the

Figure 37. Front-Lawn demonstration 1975: the speaker is Frank Stilwell.

political economy situation is unusual: regular student-staff meetings, particularly for first year undergraduates, continue to this day to be a feature of departmental decision-making.

The two imperfections in the system of professorial power that were significant in the dynamics of the political economy dispute involved faculty boards and the Senate. Both were important arenas where dissident views that challenged the authority of the professors of economics could get a hearing and have an influence.

The faculties sit in the hierarchy between departments and the Academic Board (broadened in membership from its predecessor, the Professorial Board, in 1975, but still dominated by the professoriate). Faculties had, traditionally, been relatively democratic institutions, with a membership including all full-time lecturing staff. A small number of student representatives was included. Importantly, faculties elected their own deans (a provision that ceased in the late 1980s when deans appointed by the Vice-Chancellor became the norm). It was during political economist Geelum Simpson-Lee's term of office as dean of the Faculty of Economics, after having been elected in 1972, that proposals emanating from the dissident political economy staff often received official support.

The presence of the Department of Government and Public Administration, as well as that of the Departments of Economic History (before it was disbanded in 2002) and Industrial Relations (now called Work and Organisational Studies), also gave the Faculty of Economics a broader spectrum of opinion than is typical in commerce or business faculties elsewhere. Faculty decisions in the 1970s in particular challenged the conservatism of the Department of Economics and the University establishment. The faculty meetings were often stormy affairs, with lively debates, intense lobbying and many closely contested votes. The political economists sometimes won those votes with the support of people in cognate departments, even occasionally the odd lecturer from subjects such as accounting or commercial law. It was through the intervention of the Faculty of Economics in the early 1970s that the political economy courses were established. It was also because of the partial erosion of support at this level that more reactionary elements in the Faculty, led by Stephen Salsbury, were able to drive degree restructuring intended to sideline the political economy courses in the 1980s.

As for the Senate, different considerations apply. Its constitution ensures that it is a partly elected and partly appointed decision-making body: there are elected representatives of staff, students and graduates alongside the state government's and parliament's appointees and two *ex-officio* members, the Chancellor and Vice-Chancellor. In practice, the Senate has been characteristically deferential to the Vice-Chancellor on most strategic, financial and managerial matters. Notably though, there was nearly always a political economist on the Senate during the years of the political economy dispute, first the sacked tutor Bill Waters, then Ted Wheelwright, Rod O'Donnell and, from 1997 to 2003, Gavan Butler. These political economists were variously elected by the students, graduates and academic staff. Their presence meant that, where necessary, the political economy viewpoint could usually get a hearing. In the first year of his term on the Senate, Bill Waters would periodically leave the Senate Room to announce, through a megaphone, the confidential Senate proceedings to student activists waiting outside. More coolly, the subsequent political economists on the Senate contributed to the advocacy of progressive university policy positions. More often than not, however, the current was flowing in the opposite direction.

The University's decision-making arrangements have undergone significant changes since the heyday of the political economy dispute. In the 1990s they became increasingly centralised, with more power being concentrated in the hands of a managerial elite centred on the Vice-Chancellor, Deputy Vice-Chancellors and Pro-Vice-Chancellors. Deans again came to be appointed by the Vice-Chancellor rather than elected by members of the faculties. Even professors (now including people promoted to full professorial status as well as holders of established chairs) came to have a rather more marginal status in decision-making processes, unless they were also appointed by the dean as head of their discipline. The democratic dimension of faculty decision-making arrangements had all but disappeared by the start of this century. Under the deanship of Peter Wolnizer, the infrequent meetings of the Faculty of Economics and Business were mostly taken up by the dean's own perorations. A faculty management committee, with not even a veneer of democratic composition or procedure, bolstered the dean's autonomy. 'Top-down' decision-making came to eclipse the earlier possibilities of 'bottom-up' academic rank-and-file initiatives. It was symptomatic that the decision in 2007 to transfer the Discipline of Political Economy (together with Government and International Relations) to the Faculty of Arts was not even debated at a faculty meeting.

During the heyday of the political economy dispute there was also significant conflict between the different elements within the University's power structure (each of which then had greater autonomy), as described in chapters 1–6 of this book. Bruce Williams as Vice-Chancellor did not act to implement the recommendations of the University's committees of investigation into the dispute: he refused to implement the 1974 recommendation of the Faculty of Economics that a separate Department of Political Economy be created and he declined to implement the 1976 recommendation of a committee of the Academic Board that a Unit of Political Economy be created. In 1983 the Academic Board and Senate were deadlocked over the proposal for a common introductory economics course to

Figure 38. Political economy student protesters on the stairs outside the Senate Room in 1975.

replace Economics I(P). In 1985 the restructuring of the degrees in the Faculty of Economics that was initiated by the dean, Stephen Salsbury, was contrary to the principal recommendations of the committee that reported to the Academic Board in 1982.

For their part, the political economists did not make life easy for the senior University authorities. However, the authorities themselves showed disregard not only for the interests of political economy staff and students but also for the recommendations of the University's own properly constituted committees. A charitable view would be that accommodation to the views of the various interested parties ('stakeholders', in modern managerial parlance) militated against decisive outcomes. A less charitable view is that there was institutional failure in the management of conflict.

Figure 39. Former Vice-Chancellor Bruce Williams (centre) unconvincingly suggested 'letting bygones be bygones' at the 1995 ceremony at which two of the political economists (Butler and Stilwell) collected their 25-year service medals.

Recollections of the learning experience: Sally Edsall

Political economy student activist in the 1970s; now research officer for the Teachers' Federation of New South Wales

A public school kid on a teacher education scholarship, in a world free of HECS and the necessity to have a family trust to bankroll the fees, I arrived at Sydney Uni in 1975, a working-class kid who benefited from a period when the Labor Party still had a soul. I had a penchant for reading the *Nation Review*, an interest in politics and a history of endlessly questioning the assumptions we were meant to adopt in order to achieve HSC economics success.

As I walked from Redfern Station to enrol at Maclaurin Hall, I wondered what was the meaning behind the 'Reinstate David Hill' signs painted and chalked on footpaths and across the City Road footbridge. (Has David Hill ever wondered what would have become of the New South Wales state rail system, the ABC and Soccer Australia if he had been reinstated as a tutor?) It took about half a day to connect with some like-minded people and find out the story behind the slogans.

As with so many of my other epiphanies, the one I had about political economy probably happened on the Front Lawn, or maybe it was on the steps of Fisher Library. I realised that I had to undo my Economics I enrolment and switch to the enigmatically coded Economics I(P). So, I went back to Maclaurin Hall, where I was assured that the Department of Education would accept that bracketed (P) when credentialing me as a social science (economics/geography) bonded teacher sometime in the future.

Some of the strongest friendships, as well as future professional destinies, grew from that day, an experience common to many from their uni days. As well, my involvement in the political economy struggle was the genesis of my future political activities and has remained with me through my working life.

I became a secondary teacher, but taught economics for only one year. Early on, I became an activist for the Teachers' Federation (TF) where, since 1995, I have been working as a research officer. The union is one of the few remaining advocates of social justice and equity after the Hawke, Keating and Howard periods. Some of my ongoing responsibilities include political, social and economic analyses of the actions of federal and state governments, as well as calumnies such as the GATS (General Agreement on Trade in Services) perpetrated by international bodies and governments. I love communicating understandings to TF members of such issues as the impact of the trade in services on public education and the creation of markets in education.

As a member of the Students' Economics Society when it was under the control of the political economists, I was involved in organising study and lecture days for HSC students, which makes organising a TF conference, such as the one entitled 'Economics versus the People', a doddle, given the vastly superior resources this organisation has compared with those at the disposal of us in that tiny little students' society room in the Merewether Building. I am proud of the grounding in analysis I received, which even now pops up in publications such as the *Lobby Kit*, prepared for the TF and community members for lobbying state politicians prior to the 2003 election.

I have many vivid memories from my time as a political economy student. They include giving a rousing address to students in a packed Geography II lecture about why they should support the 1976 political economy strike—and finding 100 per cent of them did. I also remember the year we all had to do Economics III because there was no Economics III(P) and the section containing the political economy questions was mysteriously left off the paper. I learnt to look with contempt upon Tony Abbott at a very early age. I remember sitting up on overnight trains to Melbourne and Adelaide to attend political economy conferences. I visited China in May 1978 as part of a group organised by Associate Professor Ted Wheelwright, and there surviving about thirty denunciations of the Gang of Four—euphemistically called 'brief introductions'—at various factories, communes, medical and educational institutions. I remember occupying the Vice-Chancellor's office during the political economy strike and being outraged that the police might be called onto a university campus to remove students.

I also recall numerous economics smokos in the Merewether Building—need I say more? Anyone who was there will know what they were about. An incognito band 'The Aints' played more than once, as I recall (better known to the New Wave/Punk crowd as The Saints).

There's much to be said for a grounding in university activism, and I highly recommend it. When it is accompanied by a spirit of scholarship and enquiry of the highest standard—the hallmark of all the courses offered through political economy—then it is something to be treasured. There is no room for complacency and inertia in this world, where the fundamental tenets of open and free enquiry and human rights sometimes assumed to have been won are openly breached and challenged every day.

One of the most popular songs through my partying days at Sydney Uni with political economy friends was Tom Robinson Band's 'Power In The Darkness', its verses each ending with the call 'Stand up and fight for your rights'. Political economy seemed like the power in the darkness at that time, and it is certainly needed now.

Figure 40. Political economy demonstration in the Quad in the 1980s.

9
Intellectual suppression

Important issues of principle—the nature of economics, progressive teaching practices and contributions to the wider society and political processes—have all been at stake in the political economy dispute at the University of Sydney. The dispute has also had its seamy side, including abuses of personal and institutional power and their consequential adverse impacts. No doubt there were regrettable behaviours by people from all camps during the confrontations that occurred, particularly in the 1970s and 1980s. However, from the political economists' perspective, the most pervasive problem was the misuse of power by those in control over administrative arrangements, resources, staffing and courses. Power inequalities invariably breed tension and resentment unless the power is used responsibly and sensitively.

How were the inequalities of power among the participants in the political economy dispute manifest? A number of practices by those in authority, from the professors of economics right up to the Vice-Chancellor, impeded the teaching and development of political economy. Notwithstanding the reservations of those powerful persons about the legitimacy of political economy and the assertive means by which it was being advanced, some of these practices were incompatible with the principle that a university should provide for free intellectual exchange and a liberal education. This is what is meant by intellectual suppression. At the University of Sydney it had a contradictory character. On the one hand, political economy *was* taught and studied there, whereas at most other universities it did not gain a foothold. In this respect the University of Sydney deserves due recognition for its capacity to accommodate strongly-supported dissenting views. On the other hand, suppression was manifested in an array of detailed practices, including opposition to course development, discrimination against staff and unfair treatment of students.

Opposition to course development was fundamental. The initial refusal by the professors of economics to permit the introduction of political economy courses was a constraint on the choice available to students and on the ability of academic staff to teach in concert according to their judgements of what comprised the most important subject matter. Was this done to maintain educational quality? No doubt those opposing the political economy proposals thought they were defending educational standards. However, the proposed curriculum reforms came from professional economists, most with PhDs and ranging in status up to associate professor. They had their own commitments to quality and to progress in the development and teaching of economics as a discipline. The resistance by the professors of economics and their supporters raises profound questions about whether the cherished university norm of academic freedom had sufficient purchase in practice.

As described in chapters 1–6, the initial opposition was to the proposals for reform of the core economics curriculum and then to subsequent proposals for first- and second-year undergraduate courses in political economy, which students could take as an alternative. Even after those alternative courses were introduced and endorsed by the Faculty of Economics and the Academic Board there was continued opposition to proposals for further course developments that would have provided an integrated undergraduate program and the possibility of extensions into honours and postgraduate work. Throughout the 1970s and early 1980s dissident political economy staff were generally prevented from introducing whole year options (which were the norm before the University changed to semesters), which meant a lack of sequential studies for students wanting to proceed beyond the second-year political economy course.[36]

The most persistent antagonism regarding course developments was towards a proposal from Evan Jones entitled 'Capital, Labour and the State'. This course proposal, first developed in 1977, sought to develop in greater depth the subject matter of the general second-year political economy course, particularly the character of economic power. Despite frequent revision by its proponent, the proposal was rejected by a majority vote of the Department of Economics staff in an almost annual ritual over a six year period, without any suggestion from the professors of economics as to the possible intellectual limitations of the course proposal or how it might be improved for future presentation.[37] It took intervention by a higher authority, the Academic Board, for a variant of the course to be introduced, which it eventually was in 1984.

The fate of another course proposal highlights the fundamentally political character of decisions regarding syllabus developments. In 1979,

---

[36] One exception was an option proposed by Frank Stilwell in his own principal field of research expertise (Regional and Urban Economics) that was accepted as part of the package imposed on the Department of Economics by the Faculty of Economics between 1975 and 1977.

[37] Academic staff in the Department of Government and Public Administration also opposed the proposal because the course content threatened their claimed monopoly of interdisciplinary analysis. The fundamental concept of power, for example, was to be purely within its bailiwick. An October 1982 letter to Warren Hogan from the Department of Government confirmed this position, implying that nothing of consequence happened within the economics discipline and that its senior luminaries were happy for this dismal state to continue.

Ted Wheelwright proposed a third-year undergraduate economics option, 'Transnational Corporations and the World Economy', which he supported with a comprehensive twenty-four page subject outline and list of readings. In a rare display of equanimity, and recognising Wheelwright's status and undoubted expertise in this subject area, some of the 'middle ground' staff in the Department voted to support the proposal when it was presented to a department meeting, tipping the balance in favour of a bare departmental majority. The department head at that time was Peter Groenewegen. He recorded the majority support for Wheelwright's course proposal, but subsequently sought and gained the University registrar's support for a reinterpretation of the meaning of 'majority', the base being redefined to include all staff in the department, whether present or not. By this definition, any members of staff absent or on leave were deemed automatically to be against any proposal presented to a department meeting.

The upshot was that Wheelwright's proposal was held not to have the necessary majority support. By way of compensation for this sleight of hand, Wheelwright was offered half of the teaching space in an existing elective (an advance on the original offer of a third), which had become vacant because its teacher was absent on study leave. The process was blatantly obstructive and the end result was a muddling of the syllabus. Years later, in 1983, the intervention of the Academic Board facilitated the introduction of a new option, 'Australia and World Capitalism', in which Wheelwright's material could be more sensibly accommodated. It was introduced as part of the deal that also required the termination of the distinct first-year course in political economy.

The development of a political economy program for honours students was another major problem. During the nine years after the introduction of undergraduate political economy courses in 1975, the fourth-year honours program in the Department of Economics had not been significantly changed. Various proposals for electives in Advanced Political Economy were made in the 1970s and early 1980s, but it became clear that, as a matter of principle, no honours seminars in political economy would be acceptable to the professors of economics. Some of the staff in the Political Economy Group had taught other orthodox economics electives in the honours program in the early 1970s[38] but, since the introduction of the new political economy courses in first and second year, only the most marginal involvement of the political economists in the honours program was tolerated. This applied to involvement in the supervision and examination of honours theses, as well as to the conduct of seminars. The inequity of this situation led the Academic Board in 1983 to identify the lack of honours electives, taught and supervised by the political economy staff, as one of the matters needing to be remedied (as it was, eventually, in 1985).

Discrimination against staff was a corollary of the opposition to the development of political economy courses during the dispute. Reference has been made in chapters 1 and 2 to the professors of economics terminating the employment of four tutors who took critical stances. Tutors on short-term contracts are easy to let go when their contracts come up for renewal. For academic staff at the level of lecturer or above, the situation is more complicated: evidence of inappropriate discrimination must necessarily be indirect since the information available to promotion and tenure committees is confidential. That having been said, the pattern seemed remarkably consistent. Almost without exception, staff in the Political Economy

---

[38] For example, Evan Jones taught welfare economics, Frank Stilwell taught microeconomics, and Gavan Butler taught development economics, turning the latter into an innovative interdisciplinary program in conjunction with Michael Leigh, a lecturer in the Department of Government and Public Administration.

Group at the University of Sydney had greater difficulties throughout the 1970s and 1980s in getting appointment, tenure and promotion than did their more orthodox colleagues.

The claim of persistent discrimination was made in a letter to the Vice-Chancellor in September 1981, written by Simpson-Lee and Wheelwright, who drew on their long experience as members of tenure and promotion committees. It read in part as follows:

> We have served on most of the tenure and promotions committees over the last ten years, and we are deeply concerned and much troubled by the way tenure/promotions procedures have been exploited by the Professors of Economics to block the progress of political economy staff, and the way tenure/promotions committees have allowed themselves to be used. The result has been unconscionable persecution of young academics at a time when they are highly vulnerable personally, in terms of their careers as academics, and their self-esteem as teachers and scholars.

Of the dissident staff, all except one were tenured by the time the political economy dispute erupted in the early 1970s. The one without tenure, Evan Jones, achieved it after six years (then a record for the University) and four successive annual applications, while a mainstream economics lecturer appointed at the same time and possessing no obviously superior qualities obtained his tenure at the end of the normal three-year probationary period.

The speed of promotion of lecturers within the Department of Economics also showed no obvious parallel with their achievements in terms of the formal criteria of research, teaching and administration. Regarding research, much has commonly been made of quality and allegations of a lack thereof; but quality has evidently been defined in terms of the method and vision of mainstream economics. It seems that the work of the political economists—as assessed from the mainstream viewpoint—must in principle be of poor quality.

Hiring procedures also left much to be desired. Successive heads of the Department of Economics refused to allocate new lecturing positions to the political economy program during the 1970s and early 1980s. There was, typically, no support from mainstream economists for the replacement of political economists when they retired. When Simpson-Lee retired in 1981, for example, there was discussion at a departmental meeting about how the vacancy should be advertised: stated opinions ranged from the vapid 'We want the best person for the job, irrespective of field of interest' to the more explicit 'There is already an excess supply of political economists'. Notwithstanding that the University was in turmoil with protests by political economy students over the denial of their interests, the selection committee recommended the appointment of a mainstream mathematical economist to replace Simpson-Lee. The predictable result was a rise in the student:staff ratio in the political economy program, to the extent that, by 1983, the student load per staff member in political economy had increased to nearly twice the level prevailing in the rest of the Department of Economics.

The appointment of professors was another focus of concern. In 1975, Wheelwright was passed over in the consideration of applications for a chair (as he had been on five previous occasions). His appointment to a full professorship would have been a major threat to the existing duopoly of Professors Simkin and Hogan. The selection committee for the vacant chair was made up of mainstream economists and other conservatives (except for Simpson-Lee, as dean), many of whom were known for their lack of empathy with the character of Wheelwright's intellectual contribution. The successful applicant's record of publications and influence was relatively slight when compared with Wheelwright's (although, having already been a professor in the UK, he was evidently appointable). Wheelwright was author or co-author of half a dozen books and editor of a plethora of collections of essays, had broad overseas experience and supporting references from six economists of international professorial stature, including the distinguished political economists Joan Robinson and John Kenneth Galbraith. He had served on two government committees of inquiry—into the future of Australian manufacturing industries and the procurement policies of government—and was on the Board of the then publicly-owned Commonwealth Bank of Australia. The Sydney Association of University Teachers (SAUT) called for an official investigation into the University's decision not to appoint Wheelwright. So too did a petition from forty members of parliament. A long and emotive exchange in the press, including overseas coverage, was generated by this affair, but it was transformed into a debate on the freedom of universities from outside interference. The University authorities thereby deflected the public outcry.

Whereas that 1975 professorial appointment was decided *in camera*, the next professorial selection process was more open. It followed the retirement of Professor Colin Simkin in 1980. Non-professorial staff had managed to secure more participation in departmental procedures by that time and, with the support of the dean of the Faculty, the staff of the Department of Economics played a significant role in the consideration of the short-listed applicants, by examining their *curriculum vitae* and conducting interviews. The procedure was careful and, given the predictable intellectual differences among the academic staff, involved substantial compromise. The official university selection committee, on first meeting, expressed support for hiring the candidate recommended by the non-professorial staff in the Department of Economics. However, after Stilwell, the one political economist on the committee, had gone overseas on study leave, the committee was recalled by its chair, Vice-Chancellor Williams. Its previous decision was reversed and the post was offered to Peter

Groenewegen who, while well qualified in research and teaching, was also widely known for his alignment with Professor Hogan against the Political Economy Group.

In these two instances the professorial appointment process was compromised by at least two undesirable practices: first, the seeming disregard of appropriate criteria for appointment (research, teaching, public service, referees' reports) in the interests of denying a political economist the rank of full professor, and second, the making of a professorial appointment in direct opposition to the academic staff's considered collective opinion. The professoriate thereby reproduced itself by a procedure in which liberal decision-making practices and due regard for a broader vision of economics were casualties.

Unfair treatment of students was a third, particularly disturbing, feature of the conflict. On the positive side, the existence of courses in political economy for first- and second-year students at the University of Sydney from the mid 1970s onwards sheltered the more questioning, assertive and non-conformist students from the problems such students have commonly experienced in economics departments elsewhere. They faced no personal discrimination when they assayed critical responses to curricula and teaching practices, at least while they were enrolled in political economy studies. Thus, in a general sense, it may well be that the problems facing dissident students of economics were, and are, less prevalent at the University of Sydney than at other universities.

The main discrimination during the political economy dispute was institutional rather than personal. It was the denial to economics students of the opportunity to study alternative political economic views in the core courses in economics in the early 1970s, and then the denial to political economy students until the early 1980s of opportunities to study in third-year and honours courses comparable with those available to students taking mainstream economics courses.

This institutional inequality made for particular problems for political economy students intent on doing honours in spite of the lack of a suitable program of studies for them. Michael Brezniak received particularly shabby treatment. Brezniak was a brilliant student who had been a prominent leader of the political economy student protest movement in the early 1970s, a principal organiser of the first national political economy conference and co-author (with Jock Collins) of the lead article in the very first issue of the *Journal of Australian Political Economy*. As noted in chapter 2, he had been suspended from the university midway during his studies for leading the noisy group of student protesters who interrupted a lecture in one of Warren Hogan's courses. The disciplinary proceedings against him through the University's Proctorial Board (which was chaired, in this instance, by Associate Professor Ken Buckley) did not result in a significant penalty being imposed. When Brezniak finished his degree, however, he was awarded a class of honours below that which he might reasonably have expected on the basis of his previous grades. His marks fell short of first-class standard in two of his five honours units of study, and it was later revealed that these papers had both been assessed by Professor Simkin, despite the fact that he had not been involved in teaching one of those two units. As a result Brezniak was not awarded the first-class honours degree.

Another difficult situation arose in 1978 when two students who had done the political economy courses in their first and second years of study chose to write theses during their final honours year in the Department of Economics. Students doing honours in this department ostensibly had a choice between taking seminars only or taking fewer seminars and writing a thesis. There was really no choice for political economy students, however, because the seminars were largely in mainstream economics. But to write a thesis was to fly in the face of the strong discouragement of the professors of economics (because 'students don't know enough to be able to write theses'). To write a thesis with a political economic orientation was particularly hazardous. One of the two students who opted to do so (exploring Michal Kalecki's political economic analysis) was given third-class honours, a decision that resulted mainly from Simkin's adverse personal judgement of the student's thesis. Requests for a procedure to process a political economy staff member's complaint of a *prima facie* case of discrimination were refused. The student went on to a successful career in the public service, but the episode showed the lack of safeguards against the possibility of discrimination in the examination procedures within the Department of Economics.

Not surprisingly, subsequent students studying political economy typically chose not to attempt honours in economics while no fourth-year political economy seminars existed, opting instead for honours in cognate departments such as Economic History, Industrial Relations and Government. The situation loosened up a little in 1986 when an elective seminar on Advanced Political Economy was introduced (as an outcome the course reforms imposed by the Academic Board on the Department of Economics) and five students were able to do coursework and theses under the supervision of staff in the Political Economy Group in that year. A fully distinct honours program in political economy was established in 1990 (flowing on from the creation of the BEc(SocSc) degree): so the problem of structural disadvantage was belatedly resolved, which led to a substantial number of excellent political economy honours theses being researched and written over subsequent years.

If one treats people dismissively and sets aside their considered opinions, that is not usually the end of the matter. In the case of the political economy dispute, the combination of official opposition to alternative course proposals, allegations of discrimination against dissident staff and unfair treatment of students provoked both short-term anger and long-term commitments among those seeking change. Such was the short-term anger that the dissident staff and students devoted enormous time and energy to the development of an oppositional movement. Thus were long-term commitments cemented. Articles were written, both for student newspapers and the mainstream media. Banners were painted and silk screen posters were laboriously produced. Badges saying 'Political Economy Now!' and 'Political Economy: Participation, not Duopoly' were made. Public demonstrations were organised. Special political economy T-shirts were printed. Generations of students passed through the political economy courses. The commitments endured, and eventually bore fruit.

Remembering a casualty of the struggle: Clive Hamilton

Political economy student activist in the 1970s; subsequently executive director of The Australia Institute, 1994–2007; now Professor of Public Ethics at the multi-university Centre for Applied Philosophy and Public Ethics, based at the Australian National University.

I arrived at the University of Sydney in 1975, the first year that Economics I(P) was offered by the Faculty of Economics. On 12 March, after the first week of lectures, I joined a demonstration by PE students. I remember the date because it was my birthday. There were around 100 of us and our objective was to make our views known to a group of third-year mainstream economics students who were listening to a lecture being given by a visiting professor. The lecturer was a guest of Professor Warren Hogan, whom I understood already to be the arch villain of neoclassical economics at the University.

The march was led by Michael Brezniak. Mike was tall and thin with a shock of curly dark hair. Jewish, direct, intense and universally acknowledged as the brilliant young man of political economy—indeed, of economics—at the University, Mike had consistently topped the class and was now entering his honours year. We marched to one of the big engineering lecture theatres down behind the Wentworth Building carrying a few placards and chanting.

We entered the theatre ten minutes into the guest lecture and streamed raucously down the aisles. I was right behind Mike as he approached the front bench. Quivering with rage, Hogan leant across the bench and pointedly reminded Mike of his position as an honours student.[39]

Mike and a couple of other students were suspended from the university for this incident and their reinstatement was the subject of an intense campaign. It was during this time that I began to understand something very important: ideas are powerful. I also began to understand that many people construct their identities and their place in society around their beliefs about how the world works, and new ideas that confront established belief present much more than an intellectual challenge. For those who cling to the old ideas, their very sense of self can be threatened and they will fight ferociously to defend them because their psychological integrity is at stake.

That is the reason why the establishment of a PE course was resisted so fiercely, not just by the mainstream professors whose power would be usurped, but by the conservative university establishment whose view of the world, and their vital role in it, was under siege. The University of Sydney is the training ground for the next generation of elites who occupy the positions of influence in business, the professions and government, and the worldview of the mainstream economists was central to the ideological reproduction of the system.

Although diverse in their views, the leading neoclassical economists in the department were in a contradictory position. After all, for market economists, if there was enough student demand for a different sort of economics why not let the market of ideas and the market for enrolments play itself out as the textbooks

---

[39] Ken Buckley in his autobiography is more explicit about the exact words of the alleged threat to Brezniak: see K. Buckley, *Buckley's! Ken Buckley: historian, author and civil libertarian: an autobiography*, A & A Book Publishing, Leichhardt, 2008, p. 270.

said? But I have since learnt that in the end people will override their most passionately held beliefs about how the world works when more important things are imperilled.

The reality is that the assertion of certain beliefs is frequently a cover for deeper motivations, and the more vehemently the beliefs are asserted the more likely it is that the real dispute is about something else, usually power. So in the PE dispute the political always became the personal, and we should keep in mind the enormous pressure that the academic leaders of political economy, notably Ted Wheelwright and Frank Stilwell, were put under.

Hogan's warning to Brezniak materialised when Mike was awarded a second-class honours degree (division I) rather than the first-class honours that he might otherwise have expected. A few years later Mike died by his own hand. His death was an enormous loss of talent for Australia and a tragedy for those who knew and loved him. Mike should always be remembered as one of the great champions of political economy at the University of Sydney.

Figure 41. Vice-Chancellor Bruce Williams in conversation with political economy students, including Clive Hamilton and Michael Brezniak in 1975.

10
Market forces

Political economists seek to understand the material forces—particularly the economic interests—shaping social change for better or worse. It is appropriate therefore to reflect on how the political economy dispute was affected by practical economic concerns. This chapter considers three such concerns—corporate sponsorship of universities, the recruitment of fee-paying students and graduate employment. We use the term 'corporate sponsorship' here to mean corporations supplying funds to universities (and perquisites to individual members of university staff) in exchange for acknowledgement of the corporations' social responsibility or responsible 'citizenship'. It implies a commitment to respect the prerogatives that corporate management asserts in regard to the organisation of production, the process of investment, the conduct of special research, the socialisation of prospective employees, and so on. The graduate employment issue, more generally, centres on the question of whether employers want their recruits to have instrumental knowledge and job-specific skills, or a generalist education, the ability to communicate effectively and an understanding of the processes of critical inquiry.

Corporate sponsorship can be expected to be a particularly sensitive issue in a field such as economics. While it is not unusual for academic disciplines to be characterised by sharp disagreement among their practitioners—that is, after all, a hallmark of academic freedom—the controversies within the economics discipline have reflected particular material interests and associated ideological positions. Neoclassical theory, although saying little about actually existing capitalism, has broadly suited corporate interests. It has underpinned the neoliberal ideology and policies of non-interference in corporate decisions—by unions, and by governments when they are seeking to regulate to protect small businesses, consumers and environmental movements in their relationships with corporations. (Where actual competition between corporate interests has been criticised by mainstream economists, however, corporate interests have felt some discomfort with neoclassical theory.) Radical currents within political economy commonly focus on a critique of capitalism, on economic inequalities and on the systemic role of the state, whether the ideological disposition of particular governments is left or right. More to the point, they turn the spotlight onto the explanation of the nature, uses and abuses of corporate power. The beneficiaries of the existing political economic order can therefore be expected to be particularly sensitive to the way students come to understand that order.

Although the major group antagonistic to the ambitions of political economy proponents at the University of Sydney has been an academic elite, supported by the administrative hierarchy, members of this elite have had links to the corporate sector. Professor Simkin was a founding member of the Sydney-based Centre for Independent Studies (CIS), a right-wing think tank backed by business interests. Professor Hogan was also active in the CIS as well as being a long-time adviser to the Liberal Party, a member of the Westpac Banking Corporation board and consultant to the corporate sector.

The political economists, on the other hand, have not typically had those corporate links. Ted Wheelwright's Transnational Corporations Research Centre did get financial support from an Australian industrialist concerned with unfair competition from transnational corporations. However, Wheelwright's research on transnational corporations was, more typically, regarded by corporate interests as being too critical; and he also experienced hostility from some other academics dependent on corporate funding for their research (in geology, pharmacology and engineering, for instance).[40] In general, the connections of the political economists have been not with the corporate sector but with political parties on the left, the organisations of the labour movement, and community and environmental organisations challenging the *status quo*. This may have provided fuel for Stephen Salsbury's recurrent claim that, as dean of the Faculty of Economics, he was inhibited in his corporate fundraising activities by the presence of the political economists.

Salsbury said that, potentially, he had large donors to the Faculty, ready to sign on the dotted line, but they never materialised. Was the political economy dispute to blame, as Salsbury implied? It seems unlikely. The presence of the political economists placed no obvious obstacle in the way of Peter Wolnizer's ambitions, as dean during a later period, to foster more business links for the Faculty of Economics and Business. The transformation that Wolnizer engineered—turning the Faculty into a business school—reflects a managerial perspective. One may infer that the board of advice established by Wolnizer, comprising mainly representatives of business interests, encouraged that transformation and, tacitly at least, approved the removal of the remaining elements of the social sciences from the Faculty.

The long-term effects of growing commercialism in the University, and within the Faculty of Economics in particular, are also an important part of the political economy story. When the political

---

[40] An article warning the business community about Wheelwright's research was written by R. Browning and titled, 'Opposition business fails to see,' published in *The Bulletin*, 24 November 1981, pp. 74–75.

economy struggle began in the early 1970s this orientation was not a major concern. Political and pedagogical issues, not financial considerations, defined the principal dimensions and directions of the dispute. It was Salsbury as dean, more than anyone else, who later introduced commercial imperatives to the Faculty of Economics. Along with other senior members of the Faculty, he became envious of the flow of international students into the BCom and MCom degree programs at the University of New South Wales (UNSW) and of the potential capacity at UNSW to recruit fee-paying local students. Under Salsbury's leadership, but with almost no attempt at innovation, the Faculty fashioned new degrees in order to attract some of the fee-paying international students flowing in increasing numbers from Hong Kong, Taiwan, Singapore, Malaysia and, later, Korea and the People's Republic of China. More recently, under Wolnizer, the dependence of the Faculty on course fees paid by international students as well as local students developed to previously unimaginable proportions: fee income exceeded government funding from 2000 onwards.

This commercial reorientation of the Faculty, combined with the federal government's parsimony and the university central administration's heavy taxation of the operating grant paid by the government, posed big challenges to a discipline such as political economy. Teaching local undergraduates who pay into HECS—political economy's traditional focus at the University—is not viable under the University's internal financing arrangements: it depends on the University's funding being augmented by income from other sources. Lacking the capacity to pay its way simply from available public revenue, the Discipline of Political Economy recurrently needed a transfer of fee revenue accruing from enrolments in other areas of the Faculty. That, in turn, forced the political economy staff, between 2003 and 2006, to offer course units within commercially oriented postgraduate degrees to earn fee income directly. As a reason for mounting courses, this was a far cry from what impelled the political economists to develop the original program of radical and challenging courses nearly thirty years earlier.

There was a pedagogic accompaniment to the commercialisation forced on universities by the stringency of federal government funding and enthusiastically embraced by successive deans of Economics (and, later, Economics and Business) at the University of Sydney. The designers of curricula were encouraged to act in the belief that universities should teach the detailed skills thought to be required in graduates' first jobs. This represented a marked change from the educational environment within which political economy initially had been taught. That said, it should also be acknowledged that most of the students enrolling for the Bachelor of Economic and Social Sciences degree apparently continued to be concerned—as were students in the predecessor BEc(SocSc) degree—with critical enquiry as well as with careers. The students in the Bachelor of International Studies degree, introduced in 2005, similarly appreciated the relevance of their studies to a changing world. The students in these degree programs typically have been intelligent and socially aware. Such students, and numerous others taking a BA or liberal studies degree of one sort or another, will surely continue to be attracted to enrol in political economy units of study, notwithstanding the general commercial reorientation of university education and the pressures to make university education narrowly focused rather than systematically broadening of perspective.

With the passage of time the value of the political economy program and its graduates has come to be widely accepted. It may have been understood by some in the broader community that a stultifying bias has pervaded the way economics and commerce are generally taught; and by others that a generalist education is better suited to the preparation of future leaders of the public sector and civil society.

Certainly, part of the trade union movement and many significant non-government organisations have testified to these different views of what the political economy struggle was about—a struggle for education that would fit in better with the needs of the modern workplace and society.

Political economy graduates have obtained demonstrably good jobs in a wide range of fields—public service, industry, finance, media, politics, academia, research and teaching. Some have become prominent in public life, including a former New South Wales state premier, a deputy premier, a state treasurer, ministers for housing and local government, other state government parliamentarians, a leader of the federal ALP Opposition, federal government ministers for aboriginal affairs and infrastructure, the federal public service commissioner, other senior public servants, professors in departments of economics and other social sciences, prominent businesspeople, journalists and well-known media personalities. Others have subsequently studied for postgraduate degrees, including degrees in law and in commerce and business as well as programs of the Securities Institute, and have had little trouble in doing so. Some employers have specifically sought graduates in political economy, reflecting a general preference for students who have been encouraged to develop skills in critical enquiry and communication, a breadth of perspective and personal judgement.

While students have usually been drawn to the study of political economy because it would enable them to develop the ability to think critically and reflectively about current political economic concerns, many have also been attracted by the apparent employability of a degree with the word 'economic' in its title. During the 1970s and 1980s it was an attraction that Peter Groenewegen's journalist friends, Clark and McGuinness, sought to undermine. They accused the political economy lecturers of pursuing an ill-thought-out campaign in which the students as foot soldiers would eventually be sacrificed in the trenches of unemployability.[41] In fact the students were never conscripts—they have freely chosen the courses that best fitted their interests and aspirations; and there is no evidence that graduates with majors in political economy have had any more difficulties gaining employment than have other graduates.

The push by Salsbury, Hogan and other opponents of political economy to introduce the separate BEc(SocSc) degree in the 1980s, in which to isolate political economy, may be interpreted as an attempt to undermine the market value of a political economy major relative to a mainstream economics major. If it was, that strategy also failed. Thousands of able students actively enrolled in the BEc(Social Sciences) degree throughout the 1980s and 1990s, and then, after 1999, in its successor, the Bachelor of Economic and Social Sciences. Their reasons for doing so included the integration of the social sciences implicit in the degree, the attraction of being able to study political economy along with other subjects having professional recognition (industrial relations and psychology, for example) and the opportunity to study in a program that challenges the orthodoxy. The preference for political economy may have also had something to do with the reputation of political economy teachers as being committed to students and open to pedagogic reform (a reputation often borne into the secondary schools by teachers who, as students, had studied political economy), as well as with the famously convivial social environment created by political economy students and, especially, the students' society (ECOPSoc),

Working in journalism warrants particular mention. A sizeable number of currently prominent economic journalists are former graduates of the political economy program. The career paths of many

---

[41] Some examples of their articles are listed on p. xiv.

of them were channelled courtesy of long-time *Sydney Morning Herald* economics editor Ross Gittins. Gittins is his own man who, over the last decade or so, has consistently hired his new staff from the political economy pool, as he pointed out when he presented a public lecture at the University in 2007. Such people know how to write, can draw information and ideas from disparate sources and usually have a sense of the big picture. Political economy graduates in journalistic positions are ideally placed to report on and analyse the ongoing tensions and crises thrown up within our economic system.

Indeed, discerning employers in various fields—public and private sectors and in non-government organisations—will surely continue to seek graduates who have these personal and literary skills and a capacity to think independently. The formation in 2006 of the political economy alumni society created a bridge with many of these former graduates, some of whom themselves have become employers of more recent graduates.

Figure 42. Political economy students, including Maria Barac on guitar, the Gration brothers and Adam Rorris enjoying a musical interlude in the Quad, 1983.

Keeping the PE movement flourishing: Darren Rodrigo

Political economy student 1999–2002; now Senior Policy Advisor to the Minister for Planning, New South Wales Government

Sick of being a porter carrying rich people's suitcases in a five-star hotel, I decided I needed to go to university. I had hoped to study economics, become a corporate businessperson, make mega bucks and have my bags carried for me for a change. Fortunately, it didn't work out that way. I didn't have the marks to get directly into an Economics degree but I did manage to scrape into Arts. Taking Political Economy (whatever that was) to get credit for my hoped-for second year move to Economics, I found myself sitting in lectures from (then) Associate Professor Frank Stilwell. It was here that my intellectual awakening began.

Every political economy student quickly learns that their opportunity to study alternative approaches to economics was won through the courage, struggle and sacrifice of the radical students and lecturers who went before them. Quickly, most become grateful for it. I learnt of the constant conservative attack, the struggle, the movement and, most vividly, about the storming of the clock tower, an event that has become legend. It was inspiring that my student predecessors were so passionate and driven that they literally put themselves on the line fighting for the right to study Political Economy, for the right of people like me to sit in lectures on this subject.

Fast forward to 2004 and my personal situation was not looking good. In my second year since finishing university, and with nothing to show for it but a stack of job rejection letters, I contacted my old honours thesis supervisor, (by now) Professor Frank Stilwell, looking for work or academic experience that would give me some traction in the labour market. He offered me a job tutoring in the first year Economics as a Social Science course. As well as being my first big break, this would engage me directly in the new fight for Political Economy.

We were clearly in trouble with only 260 first-year students that year, an alarming fall from a high of 400 in 2000. The diminishing student numbers gave rise to the fear that, just as Economic History had been, the Political Economy program would be wound up, a fear further fuelled by criticisms levelled by the dean of

Economics and Business that the Discipline of Political Economy was perpetually running a deficit, accusations based on a dubious funding model that penalised Political Economy for not teaching higher proportions of full fee-paying and international students. Political Economy staff who retired were not replaced. The dean broadly implied that the situation could not continue.

Yet, despite people's fears, PE at Sydney University has the unique characteristic of drawing out a deep passion and conviction that reflects the ideological commitment of its students and the way the academic staff teach. When Political Economy is attacked, current and former PE students feel themselves affronted. It is in this way that the original spirit of struggle lives on among current PE students and recent graduates who would willingly take up to fight. And so, with Frank, we made plans to go on the offensive.

We needed more students. Frank and I rewrote, redesigned and funded a PE promotional flyer—PE is a great course with great teachers—which we targeted directly at prospective first year students. At 'Sydney Uni Live!', current and former PE students hit the campus in the spirit of those radical students of the 1970s, spreading the word, putting up posters and talking to students. We didn't storm the clock tower, but on course enrolment day we did storm the long lines of Arts students in the Quad, handing out the brochures promoting political economy. It worked. In 2005 enrolments rose again to a respectable 400 first-years.

We also realised that, if Political Economy was going to survive over the longer term, it would require an organisation to harness and direct the energies and goodwill of PE graduates to achieve that objective. From this notion the Sydney University Political Economy Alumni Society was born in late 2005. Its launch at the Wentworth Building was attended by around 200 people and our guest speaker, former PE student and then ACTU national secretary Greg Combet, flew up from Melbourne for the occasion.

Although created to facilitate social events as well, the Alumni Society to date has mainly been involved in political actions in defence of Political Economy. In 2006 we lobbied the dean of the Faculty of Economics and Business about the funding and positioning of Political Economy, as the Faculty sought to divest itself of Government and Political Economy in order to become a pure business school.

We also lobbied the committee looking into the shifting of Government and PE to a proposed new school for the study of social sciences in the Faculty of Arts.

It is likely that the Alumni Society, working closely with PE staff and students in the Political Economy Students' Society, will play a critical role in ensuring that enrolment numbers are kept high and interest in studying PE is fostered and kept strong. Politically, the challenge is to guarantee that Political Economy's transition to the School of Social and Political Sciences ensures its long-term sustainability. If these goals are achieved, could this end the perpetual struggle for survival that PE had experienced in the Faculty of Economics and Business?

To those who were engaged in the struggle, and who have regrets or misgivings about the success of otherwise of the PE movement, let me say this. Whether we acknowledge it or not, Political Economy is a progressive institution on the Australian political landscape. It has shaped, and continues to shape, individuals who have gone on to make invaluable contributions to progressive causes in academia, journalism, the labour movement and politics. That achievement cannot and should not be underrated. What we did mattered and still means something.

As for the future: we are here, we remember and we remain committed.

The Political Economy Alumni Society is a network of political economy graduates that meets socially and works to promote and support the study of political economy in academia and the broader community.

Alumni Society events are open to everyone who is interested in exploring economic issues in their social and political context.

If you would like to join the Alumni Society, email Darren Rodrigo at:

darrenrodrigo@hotmail.com

11
Dissent and legitimacy

The political economy dispute reflected the social and political context in which it originated and developed. In addition to the concerns considered in the preceding chapters—subject matter, pedagogy and power, intellectual suppression and economic interests—a broader array of contingent factors shaped the development of the struggle for political economy at the University of Sydney. There was the influence of the prevailing ideas in other academic disciplines and in society more generally, the relationship to the academics' union and broader university politics, the impetus given by distinguished academic visitors, by the development of a national organisation for political economists and by the establishment of a journal to promote interest in political economy. This chapter explores these and other elements in the process of dissent and the quest for legitimacy.

The legitimacy of the political economy movement at the University of Sydney during the protracted institutional conflict was always at issue. The resort by student activists to direct action was one recurrent concern, predictably fuelling conservative reactions. Former Vice-Chancellor Williams' emphasis on this aspect of the struggle for political economy courses is indicative.[42] Indeed, some incidents were ill-considered and regrettable, including the spray painting outside his residence and some of the behaviour by militant activists making uninvited entries into his office and that of the registrar at the

---

[42] B. Williams, *Making and breaking universities*, Macleay Press, Sydney, 2005, chapter 5.

University. Law and order issues took temporary priority over the issues of educational reform as a consequence. In the longer term, however, the issue of legitimacy hinged primarily on whether the political economists had a good cause.

The alternative presented by political economy had to be shown to be useful as a means of understanding a complex and changing world. The academic staff in the Political Economy Group relentlessly pursued this theme, with some success in both teaching and publications. From the first national political economy conference onwards, there was also sustained support and assistance of some highly-regarded political economists from universities throughout the world. The program of political economy courses showed its capacity to contribute to an understanding of the economy and its social foundations that meshed with research and teaching in economic history, sociology, anthropology, industrial relations and other social sciences. From both student and staff perspectives, this relationship of political economy to cognate subjects has been a crucial element of integration and coherence.

The early 1970s saw dissent and change emerge in many of these other subjects too. In the sciences, there was a campaign for social responsibility in science. In the Department of Social Work a major dispute focused on course content and the abuse of professorial power; and it was only concluded after Stuart Rees, a new professor committed to progressive administrative and educational practices, was appointed in 1978 to replace the previous incumbent. Meanwhile, within the Faculty of Economics, Kingsley Laffer was striving to have the teaching of industrial relations separated from the Department of Economics in order to practise an interdisciplinary approach to the subject. Enthusiastic young academics in the Department of Government, including Dennis Altman, Bob Connell, Terry Irving, Lex Watson, Peter King, Michael Leigh, Ernie Chaples and Michael

Jackson, were exploring innovative practices in teaching as well as research into contemporary political issues. The Department of Fine Arts (curiously located at that time alongside the Department of Economics in the Merewether Building) included Bernard Smith, David Saunders, Terry Smith and other academic staff who were seeking to invigorate Australian art history and to promote conceptual art.

Support from colleagues in these and other academic disciplines played a significant part in the development of the political economy program. In the early days of the dispute, staff in the Department of Government (not including its professors) were particularly supportive, although a sense of solidarity slowly receded in the 1980s. Support for political economy also came from academics in the Department of Economic History (particularly Ken Buckley), and the industrial sociologists and labour historians in Industrial Relations (which the discipline was then called before it came under the influence of human resources management). Without these sources of support within the Faculty of Economics the number of the political economy staff would have been insufficient to make progress through the official channels—a necessary adjunct to the direct action by student activists that was helping to lubricate those channels.

Elsewhere in the University, the political economists received significant support, especially on the Academic Board. That some of the individual political economy staff were known for their commitment to a range of progressive causes on and off campus evidently did no harm to the reputation of the political economy movement. A couple of the political economists built up cooperative arrangements with Faculty of Arts colleagues in what eventually became a Department of Sociology, a department that was created only after the retirement of Bruce Williams as Vice-Chancellor. Williams, renowned for his opposition to creating a department of political economy, had also maintained the university's long-standing reluctance to allow a department of sociology to be established.

Other areas in which political economists developed fruitful personal links included history, philosophy, anthropology, social work, geography and urban and regional planning. This was not only a matter of shared concerns with interdisciplinary social sciences but also a matter of shared values, particularly in the context of seeking progressive reform within a generally conservative university.

The support for political economy during the early stages of the dispute also derived from struggles elsewhere. Perhaps the most important focus for dissent—even more intense for a while than the conflict in the Department of Economics—was the Department of Philosophy in the Faculty of Arts. The contest there was between academic staff and students concerned with contemporary social and political philosophy and those, typically more senior, staff who were committed to a traditional study of moral philosophy and logic, and to an emphasis on analytic philosophy. When the latter group, fed up with the continuing conflict in the Department, asked Vice-Chancellor Williams to split the two groups into separate departments, he readily agreed to do so. A Senate committee had found that there was 'an impossible atmosphere in which to carry on the affairs of any department'. The split was announced in October 1973. The names given to the two departments were General Philosophy, and Traditional and Modern Philosophy. Among the academics in General were John Burnheim, Michael Devitt, Wal Suchting, Jean Curthoys and George Molnar; in Trad. and Mod. were David Armstrong, Keith Campbell and David Stove, among others. Perhaps even more clearly than was the case in the Department of Economics, the division was broadly between staff politically on the left and those on the right, although in practice, many other elements shaped the conflict.[43]

The philosophy split set a precedent that gave heart to political economy supporters who were urging the Vice-Chancellor to create a Department of Political Economy; but, in the case of philosophy, the demand for a separate department had come from the senior professor in that department and the more conservative academic staff, not from the dissidents.

The influence of feminism was significant in the philosophy dispute, and this too provided some link with political economy. The controversial elective on the philosophical foundations of feminism that two tutors, Liz Jacka and Jean Curthoys, proposed to teach had been strongly opposed by Armstrong, Stove and their supporters. The resulting strike in 1973 involved students in many other departments (including the students in Economics I, then being taught by Stilwell), as noted previously in chapter 1. Those advocating the study of feminism argued that issues of particular importance to women had been ignored or repudiated, that the construction of gender is partly the product of political and economic processes, that gender inequalities have been (counterproductively) embedded in politico-economic structures and, ultimately, that women's liberation is also liberating of men. Although these notions were generally met with hostility among the conservative males within the University administration, the feminist philosophy elective eventually got the approval of the Faculty of Arts, with the Dean, Alex Jones, using his

---

[43] See P. Crittenden, *Changing orders: scenes of clerical and academic life*, Brandl & Schlesinger, Blackheath, NSW, 2008, pp. 306–12 and 328–46; and J. Burnheim & P. Crittenden, 'Political polarisation in Australian philosophy? The 1960s and their aftermath,' in G. Oppy & N. Trakakis (eds), *A history of Australian philosophy*, Springer, New York (forthcoming).

casting vote in favour after a tied vote. The elective was allowed to be taught by Jacka and Curthoys, formally under the supervision of Associate Professor John Burnheim.

Feminism also directly influenced the political economy movement. An elective called the Political Economy of Women was developed by Margaret Power—the one woman in the Political Economy Group during its first decade—in conjunction with three women in other departments of the University. It was presented to the Faculty of Economics for introduction as an interdisciplinary course option, starting in 1974. So it actually preceded by one year the introduction of the general first year undergraduate course in political economy, Economics I(P).

The Political Economy of Women elective could be taken by students in the Faculties of Economics and Arts within a government major, as a free-standing elective by students in the Faculty of Economics, and then (as soon as the degree restructuring allowed it) as part of a political economy major. It brought together contributions by women whose disciplinary focus was in fields such as art history, media studies, anthropology and government. At the same time, Power was urging her political economy colleagues to incorporate issues of patriarchy and gender into the core political economy courses. A concern with gender inequality did come to be an ongoing feature in those courses although it was short of what Power had been urging.[44]

---

[44] See M. Power, '21 years of the political economy of women,' paper presented at the anniversary conference of Political Economy at the University of Sydney, 22 October 1994. The influence of feminism at the university also led, later, to the establishment of the Women's Research Unit in the Vice-Chancellor's office. For recollections of this experience, see G. Poiner, 'The Women's Research Unit: being there,' *Australian Feminist Studies*, vol. 13, no. 27, 1998, pp. 91–97.

Other social and intellectual currents were also to exert an influence and to link political economy to broader social concerns. Environmentalism, like feminism, was on the rise in the 1970s, following the publication of landmark studies, such as Rachel Carson's *The silent spring* and the Club of Rome's *The limits to growth*. Its impact on the structure of the political economy program at the University of Sydney was modest at first, comprising a short series of lectures given by Stilwell in Economics I(P) and an optional tutorial stream. But after the green light was given for the development of third year units of study in political economy, an elective on the Political Economy of the Environment, taught by Stuart Rosewarne, was introduced in 1993.

Other academic appointees to political economy in the 1980s and 1990s, including Dick Bryan, Gabrielle Meagher, Pamela Cawthorne, Tim Anderson and Liz Hill, subsequently initiated other electives that focused on, for example, international finance, welfare and industry policies, corporate codes of conduct, the relationship between class and gender, and the political economy of human rights. These course developments put into more tangible form the array of concerns that had originally appeared on the political economic agenda in the 1970s.

Political economy thereby gained legitimacy by responding to the growing interest in cross-disciplinary studies, recognising that narrowly constructed disciplines, such as mainstream economics, cannot adequately understand and explain important contemporary changes.

Looked at from this perspective, the movement for political economy could be seen as partly stimulated by, and significantly contributing to, a broader movement to promote interdisciplinary social science. Therein also lie certain tensions—between breadth and depth in the teaching of political economy and between interdisciplinarity and attention to classical themes—but this was not so evident in the heyday of the political economy dispute when the narrowness and shallowness of mainstream economics were such clear targets.

Union support and university reform

The support of the academics' union was also important for the legitimacy of the political economy struggle at the University of Sydney. When the dispute was getting under way in the 1970s the relevant staff organisation was the Sydney Association of University Teachers (SAUT), which had been pushing for the democratisation of university governance, with particular focus on the transformation of the Professorial Board into an Academic Board that would include some elected non-professorial staff and students, as well as full professors and deans. The new Academic Board, established in 1975, had among its earliest elected non-professorial members some outspoken individuals, including political economists Gavan Butler and Frank Stilwell. Butler remained on the board for a great part of the next two decades, combining that with an active role on the SAUT committee, serving as secretary for SAUT from 1982 to 1985 and then as its president from 1988 to 1989.

Reforms pursued by SAUT included the election of departmental heads, following the precedent that had already been created in the election of deans. The intransigence of successive heads of the Department of Economics, when faced with proposals for the establishment of new political economy courses, was of particular concern to the committee and membership of SAUT. It highlighted the dangers arising from concentrating power among the departmental heads appointed by the Vice-Chancellor rather than in heads elected by the academic staff.

In 1976 a resolution proposing that SAUT support the demands of the political economy movement brought the union directly into the dispute in the Department of Economics. An extraordinarily well-attended SAUT meeting, packing a 400-seat Carslaw Lecture Theatre, was chaired by historian Neville Meaney. Fiery speeches were made by proponents of political economy, while strong opposition came from conservative members of the professoriate, including Professor Leonie Kramer, later to become Chancellor of the University. In the event, the resolution of support for political economy was adopted by an overwhelming majority of the members attending the meeting. That result was interpreted by the Vice-Chancellor, Bruce Williams, as a repudiation of his authority; as a result, Williams (and others among a conservative professoriate) resigned from SAUT.

SAUT remained supportive throughout the political economy struggle. The various issues that the struggle raised, including political discrimination in appointments, promotion procedures that were open to abuse, malpractice in departmental administration and professors overruling majority opinions expressed in departmental meetings, were all of broader concern to rank-and-file academics. The SAUT committee was well informed about the political economy struggle because of Butler's ongoing presence.

More recently, this tradition of direct engagement in academic union issues has been continued by other political economy staff, Stuart Rosewarne, Dick Bryan and Damien Cahill, who have been active in the University of Sydney branch of the National Tertiary Education Union, (NTEU), which replaced SAUT in the 1980s. Dick Bryan represented the union in a series of enterprise-bargaining processes. Stuart Rosewarne was president of the union's University of Sydney branch between 1997 and 2000 and then New South Wales state president between 2004 and 2008.

Nationwide organisational support for the political economy struggle was also facilitated by the formation of the Australian Political Economy Movement (APEM). The decision to form APEM emerged from the 1976 national political economy conference, which showed that the concerns of the political economists at the University of Sydney were connected to a wider academic community and broader social and political issues. Following the conference, a part-time administrator, John Cozijn, was employed by APEM to help to develop the organisation. APEM produced periodic newsletters that gave information about conferences and other events.

Well-attended conferences held in Melbourne, Adelaide, Canberra and Sydney held under the auspices of APEM over the next few years had a buzz comparable to that of the first Sydney conference. The practice of the annual conference died out in the early 1980s, however, and there have been only one-off events on a few occasions in the past two decades. A conference was held at the University of Sydney in 1994 to celebrate twenty years of political economy courses and twenty-one years of the Political Economy of Women; a smaller-scale political economy conference that focused on education in political economy was held at the University of Sydney in 2003; and a national political economy conference is to be held in Wollongong in 2009.

As an aside, it is pertinent to ask why the momentum for more regular large-scale political economy conferences such as those held in the 1970s and early 1980s was not sustained. One obvious explanation is the proliferation of events organised by other politically progressive organisations. The annual conferences of the Society for Heterodox Economics (SHE) now serve a similar function, albeit mainly for a more narrowly academic clientele.

There have also been more negative influences inhibiting the development of a national political economy movement, such as the loss of confidence in the possibility of progressive reform during the 1980s and 1990s when Labor federal governments under Prime Ministers Hawke and Keating began the embrace of economic rationalism. During the Howard government years, the dominance of neoliberal economics was stronger still. It was not uncontested, of course. The critique was carried out in other forums such as the 'Now we the people' conferences convened by the Search Foundation and the regular sessions of 'Politics in the pub'.

At the time when political economy was establishing its credentials as an alternative to mainstream economics, however, the support shown for the national political economy conferences was particularly important. The colour photos featured in this book show the posters for the conferences that were held in Sydney.

Political economy publications

Legitimacy for the political economy movement has also come through the publication of the *Journal of Australian Political Economy* (*JAPE*). The decision to launch *JAPE* grew out of discussions among political economists and activists from various states who had come together at the first national political economy conference. A special meeting of the Australian Political Economy Movement held at a hired hall in the inner Sydney suburb of Balmain resolved to initiate the journal and elected the initial editorial committee. The first issue was published in October 1977. Its editorial made somewhat grandiose claims about its aim to 'represent and encourage a social movement ... for a democratic economy, as a necessary precondition for a fully democratic society'.

JAPE was produced for its first ten years by regional collectives based in Sydney, Melbourne, Adelaide and Canberra but, as many of its founders moved on to other activities and as APEM ceased to have any function other than the publication of the journal, *JAPE* came to be managed mainly by the political economy staff group at the University of Sydney. Only at this site was there—and is there still—the necessary, enduring institutional base.

JAPE settled down to being a bi-annual publication, usually of about 160 pages, with articles on a wide range of Australian and international political economic concerns. It is aimed at a readership of progressive academics, students, union research officers, political staffers and a critically aware general public. In December 2002 the journal published its fiftieth issue. The first fifty issues had included articles contributed by 244 different authors and sixty-four book reviewers; while 210 people had been involved as referees. This is indicative of *JAPE*'s broad base of support and its role in fostering the development of studies in political economy nationwide. The sixtieth issue was published in December 2007, followed by a special issue on the Australian economic boom 1992–2008, just as the boom was ending. The online version of the journal now makes it more widely accessible nationally and internationally.[45]

---

[45] The website of the *Journal of Australian Political Economy* is www.jape.org

Other publications produced in the early years of the dispute, especially as teaching aids, were also important in gaining legitimacy for the political economy movement. Particularly important were five volumes of *Essays on the Political Economy of Australian Capitalism*, edited by Ted Wheelwright in conjunction with economic historian Ken Buckley. Wheelwright and Buckley were later to produce *No Paradise for Workers* and *False Paradise*, two books on Australian economic history from a labour perspective. Two volumes of *Readings in Political Economy*, edited by Wheelwright and Stilwell, specifically designed for use in the new political economy courses at the University of Sydney, were published in 1976. These books paved the way for the strong tradition of research and publishing by Australian political economists in the 1980s and 1990s.

Some of these subsequent publications were designed primarily for teaching. This was important, given the mainstream orientation of nearly all economics textbooks and the smaller number of alternative political economy texts. *Economics as a social science: readings in political economy*, was edited by Stilwell in conjunction with George Argyrous, a former University of Sydney political economy student who subsequently became senior lecturer at the University of New South Wales; this book first appeared in 1996, and then in a second, revised edition in 2003. Oxford University Press published a general textbook written by Stilwell for students of political economy called *Political economy: the contest of economic ideas*; its first edition appeared in 2002 and a second revised edition was published in 2006.

Publications by members of the Political Economy Group have not been limited to teaching-oriented books, of course, and have included other research-based books by Stilwell, Dick Bryan, Joseph Halevi, Gabrielle Meagher and Bill Dunn. Former political economy students, such as Clive Hamilton, Steve Keen, Rod O'Donnell, Philip Toner, Bill Lucarelli and Rick Kuhn, have also published significant books on political economic issues, some to wide acclaim.

Further legitimacy came from the subsequent visits of distinguished academic economists who were willing to be associated with the University of Sydney political economists. Professor Joan Robinson from Cambridge University came for a week in 1975, lectured to a

Dissent and legitimacy • 171

Figure 43. Professor Joan Robinson speaking on the political economy challenge at the University of Sydney in 1975.

packed Wallace Lecture Theatre, presented the R.C. Mills memorial lecture and a staff seminar, and appeared as the principal guest on ABC Television's *Monday Conference*. Professor J.K. Galbraith from Harvard University came in 1987 and accepted an invitation to present a public lecture. Stilwell, who organised the event, billed it as Galbraith launching the new BEc(SocSc) degree, which annoyed the then dean Murray Wells because, according to Wells, a degree program (as distinct from a department or faculty) cannot host a public lecture. Galbraith's eminent professional stature and literary reputation ensured a full house in the largest Merewether Lecture

Theatre.⁴⁶ Other notable political economists such as Bob Rowthorn, Rhys Jenkins, Andrew Glyn, Susan Himmelweit, Simon Mohun and Shaun Hargreaves Heap from the UK, and Makato Itoh from Japan, have come for extended visits and contributed enthusiastically to teaching political economy at the University of Sydney.⁴⁷

What about relationships within the Department of Economics? It is fair to say that legitimacy for the political economists was never established there. The conflictual relationships were not conducive to—indeed, continually denied—legitimacy. However, the situation was rather more complex than a simple polarisation between the mainstream economists and the dissident Political Economy Group. Some mainstream economists concerned with practical issues such as housing, labour markets and unemployment occasionally lent their support to proposals coming from staff in the Political Economy Group, although on key votes at department and faculty meetings, they usually supported the professors. These people, known generally as the 'middle ground', found the political economists' agenda not to their liking. Personal relationships suffered. In circumstances such as

---

⁴⁶ A bizarre episode followed Galbraith's lecture. David Clark, the journalist who had written many articles seeking to discredit the political economy courses at the University of Sydney, wrote an article in the *Australian Financial Review* claiming that Stilwell had 'kidnapped' Galbraith. In fact, Stilwell, who had chaired the meeting, left together with Galbraith in a taxi after the event and went to the hotel where Galbraith would meet his wife before going to the theatre that evening. Clark, who had sought to get Galbraith into his car instead, was evidently feeling somewhat thwarted. A complaint about Clark's fantastic misrepresentation of the events was made to the Press Council, see *Australian Financial Review*, 6 August 1987, p. 6.

⁴⁷ Galbraith and Robinson both agreed to annual prizes being given in their names to students topping political economy courses, as did Paul Sweezy and Gunnar Myrdal. Prizes in honour of Ted Wheelwright and Geelum Simpson-Lee were later added.

those obtaining in the Department of Economics during the years of rebellion, those who choose to rebel implicitly rebuke those who do not. There were also explicit rebukes from time to time.

Relationships with mainstream Australian economists beyond the University of Sydney also remained poor. This was not for want of attempts at dialogue. Stilwell and Butler contributed a paper to the 1976 national conference of the Economics Society of Australia and New Zealand, explaining the nature of the political economists' approach to the discipline and its teaching. Evan Jones presented another paper on economic methodology at the same conference, and persisted over many years with making presentations at the society's subsequent conferences. Jones and Stilwell, seeking to engage with the discipline and its conventional practitioners, also published articles on the political economic challenge to mainstream economics in *Economic Record*, the Economics Society's principal journal. Stilwell was still at it in 2005, presenting a paper at the Australasian Teaching Economics Conference on how a political economy curriculum and a pluralist pedagogy can challenge mainstream economics and make the educational process more fulfilling.[48] Yet mainstream economists in Australia, with minor individual exceptions, were evidently unwilling to pick up the gauntlet thrown down by the political economists. They seem to have regarded political economy either as an irrelevance or an unwelcome threat.

---

[48] See G.J. Butler & F. Stilwell, 'The revival of political economy,' *Economics*, 1976, pp. 15–24; E. Jones, 'Positive economics or what?' *The Economic Record*, vol. 53, no. 143, September 1977, pp. 350–63; F. Stilwell, 'Political economy: common and contested terrain,' *The Economic Record*, vol. 64, no. 184, March 1988, pp. 14–25; and F. Stilwell, 'Teaching political economy: curriculum and pedagogy,' *Australasian Journal of Economics Education*, vol. 2, no. 2, September 2005, pp. 66–82.

Professional marginalisation within academia persists. The mainstream economists generally don't want to know. When Ross Gittins gave his talk at the University in 2007 about the limitations of conventional economics, the economics students came in large numbers but their lecturers were conspicuous by their absence. Similarly, one might have expected the publication of *Debunking economics: the naked emperor of the social sciences* by Steve Keen (the former political economy student activist who became associate professor of economics at the University of Western Sydney) to have provoked more interest and responses from mainstream economists than it did. Rather than explicitly defending the orthodoxy, it is evidently easier just to ignore the critics and carry on regardless.

Some broader professional recognition has eventually come to the scholarly contributions of individual political economists, however. Several, including Dick Bryan, Stuart Rosewarne and Frank Stilwell, have been successful in winning research grants from the Australian Research Council and other grant-awarding bodies, as was Gabrielle Meagher when she was in the Discipline of Political Economy. The Academy of the Social Sciences in Australia elected Stilwell to a Fellowship in 2000, just before he was promoted to a personal professorship, becoming the first professor of political economy at an Australian university in modern times.[49]

Ultimately, the legitimacy of political economy rests on the usefulness of the alternatives it offers to mainstream economics in attempting to understand economic systems. The situation is complicated by the presence of differences about those political economic alternatives. The political economists at the University of Sydney—and in the

---

[49] Political economists Geoff Harcourt and Herb Thompson had previously been appointed to chairs in *economics* at the University of Adelaide and Murdoch University respectively.

global political economic community—have engaged in robust discussions with each other on matters of theory, method, research direction and teaching practices. There is no monolithic body of political economic thought, or any necessary agreement on strategic judgements about how best to challenge the orthodoxy within economics.

During the more than three decades since the political economy dispute began, the political economy staff themselves have aired different views on a range of issues, including how the courses should be constructed and developed. Interpreting political economy as non-neoclassical economics opens up diverse schools of thought. The original group of dissident staff emphasised the Marxian tradition, along with institutional, feminist and post-Keynesian approaches to political economic analysis. The range of approaches among the current political economists is no less.[50]

This diversity of viewpoints has made for lively internal debates. By the same token, the possibility that differences of approach may lead to internal incoherence within team-taught courses or across the political economy program as a whole has been a recurrent concern. Thus, periodically, there have been reconsiderations of program structure and of units of study, especially those at the core of the undergraduate program, and consequent restructurings. Team-taught courses have tended to give way to units of study for which individual lecturers have responsibility.

---

[50] This diversity of viewpoints is illustrated by some of the articles in the *Journal of Australian Political Economy*, e.g. by Gavan Butler, Stuart Rosewarne, Tim Anderson and Dick Bryan in issue no. 50 and by Anderson (with a response by Don Munro) in issue no. 54; see also Stilwell, 'Four reasons for pluralism in economics,' *Australasian Journal of Economics Education*, vol. 3, nos. 1-2, 2006, pp. 42-55.

The balance between the advantages of diversity and its potential for disunity is always hard to strike. This was particularly problematic during the period 2005–7 when there were tensions among the academic staff because of the threats to the survival of the Discipline of Political Economy within the Faculty of Economics and Business. Being on the cusp between critical social science and business studies posed particular challenges for Political Economy. As the Faculty of Economics and Business was transformed, in effect, into a business school this tension came into particularly sharp relief. Significant differences developed among the Political Economy staff about how best to respond to these changing conditions. The University's decision to create the new School of Social and Political Sciences in the Faculty of Arts at the start of 2008 created the necessary resolution: the political economists agreed on the need to grasp the opportunity. As one door closes another opens …

The relocation of political economy can also be expected to have a major bearing on its perceived legitimacy in the years ahead. Being in the Faculty of Arts separates political economy to a greater extent, institutionally, from mainstream economics. This creates a different context to that which gave rise to the political economy dispute three decades previously. On the one hand, it makes the political economists' challenge to orthodoxy easier for the mainstream economists to ignore. On the other hand, the new location creates more possibilities for the political economists to teach economics as a social science, to forge connections with teachers and researchers in cognate social sciences and to build a strong reputation beyond the constricted and self-referential field of mainstream economics.

The Department of Political Economy certainly got off to a good start in its new home. Undergraduate student enrolments hit a record level in the first year. Postgraduate enrolments surged in the next. An official Faculty of Arts review set up by the dean, and undertaken by three distinguished academics from Melbourne, Canada and Sydney, assessed the department in late December 2008. Its report, presented in February 2009, complimented the department on its high standards of excellence in teaching and emphasised its potential to build a yet stronger profile as a nationally and internationally renowned centre for the study of political economy.

Figure 44. Ironic cartoon in *Honi Soit* in 1975 accompanying an article about the extraordinary difficulty experienced by dissident lecturer Evan Jones in obtaining tenure.

Recollections of emergent radicalism: Rick Kuhn

Political economy student activist in the 1970s; now Reader in Political Science at the Australian National University

My politics germinated at Sydney Uni in the mid-1970s. The student revolution, a rich medium of overlapping struggles, discussions and commitments, lasted longer there than at most other Australian universities. The campaign for political economy courses was the struggle that did the most to keep the soil of student revolt fertile during those years.

My memories of the movement for political economy are now thin and fragmented. My diaries indicate that I became involved during my first year at uni, 1974. Very interested in politics, though without much politics of my own, my first involvement was with the experiment in participative management going on in the Government department. But the tedium of Economics I, the enthusiasm of existing activists in the political economy campaign and the large mobilisations drew me into the PE movement.

Experience with the Students' Representative Council, the Australian Union of Students and various official university bodies over the next couple of years helped me develop useful skills in debate, caucusing and the negotiation of bureaucratic structures. But participating in different campaigns which involved (or at least tried to involve) large numbers of students, especially the PE movement, demonstrated that real politics was about mobilising people to shape their world. The other stuff could be important, but only to the extent that it contributed to the struggle. This was not a conclusion I consciously worked out at the time. But it was an experience that became central to my politics.

Between 1974 and 1976, often hundreds and sometimes thousands of students were active in the movement. It was not only positive personal experiences, but also mistakes I made that that led me to assimilate the idea that change was crucially the product of mass action and militancy.

I chaired a large Front-Lawn meeting during the height of the campaign in 1975 and, as agreed beforehand, proposed that we should all deliver our message to the Vice-Chancellor in person. The locked office seemed to put an end to our plans, but, thankfully, others were less intimidated by the solid timber door. Martin Hirst, in particular, showed that it need not be a barrier at all.

The PE campaign provided experiences of political practice as struggle. A *Capital* reading group, which included economics and philosophy undergraduates, postgraduate students and tutors, developed my understanding of Marxist theory. Vocal members of the group, among them Jock Collins, Paul Patten, Theresa Brennan and Peter King, were older and wiser than me; the most sophisticated members were into Louis Althusser's interpretation of Marx. The group was a stimulating environment, where a relative beginner could grasp what Marx was on about. I was already a junior Althusserian.

The experience of the group was sometimes chemically facilitated. One evening, the dope overwhelmed my keen interest in the labour theory of value. The others were apparently unaffected by what seemed to me to be a stunningly potent deal as they learnedly discussed difficult passages in Volume I while coloured wavy lines wafted through the air before my eyes. After the meeting, we went, as usual, to the Forest Lodge Hotel. I gave a couple of people a lift in my car over the short distance from the Quad to the pub. This was a foolish thing to do, in my ripped state. The others went in, after I had parked, one wheel up on the kerb. After a half hour nap, certainly not punctuated by dreams of C+V+S, I had come down enough to join the discussion in the bar. Despite this episode, quite a lot of the economic and political implications of *Capital* did sink in.

I played a small role in helping to organise the first Australian political economy conference in June 1976. In addition to other tasks, Bruce Lanahan and I undertook to produce a T-shirt for the conference. The organising committee rejected our first design proposal, which featured Jiang Ching, Mao's wife. For us, she was a rather abstract and quirky symbol for very hard Left politics. The committee's decision led to a vastly superior conference product, both in terms of politics and humour. Without consulting the committee further, we used a cartoon frame of Phineas Freak saying, 'An' when yer smashin' th' state, kids … don't fergit t' keep a smile on yer lips an' a song in yer hearts'.

Thanks to Trevor Matthews, who taught in the Government department, I got a job in the public service in Canberra in 1977 with the Committee of Inquiry into Education and Training, chaired by Bruce Williams, University of Sydney Vice-Chancellor.

During 1976, Lanahan had been invited to talk to a socialist organisation about the PE struggles. He took me with him. This was my first contact with the International Socialists (IS), whose contemporary descendant is Socialist Alternative. I wasn't impressed by this handful of revolutionaries in a seedy Summer Hill flat.

In Canberra, I missed the stimulating political atmosphere of Sydney Uni, particularly political discussion. The Canberra branch of IS seemed much more appealing than the Sydney one. And, once I learnt a bit about the IS's politics, I found them very attractive. The group was sober about its own significance and the state of Australian society. Its emphasis that Marxism was about the self-emancipation of the working class matched the belief in the power of mass action and militancy that I had assimilated from being involved in the PE movement. It seemed the good stuff was actually in Marx, rather than Althusser. I joined the IS.

In 1983, the PE struggle had revived in the face of a decision by conservative economics professors and the Academic Board to abolish the courses. Back at Sydney Uni to do a PhD in the Government department, I became involved again and wrote an IS leaflet about the dispute, which included a PE song from 1975. With less art but a broader empirical content than Dylan's, the lyrics expressed the spirit of the movement at its peak, that I found generalised in wider, revolutionary socialist politics.

Come gather round students wherever you are
And complain that your courses are outdated by far,
And demand with professors you're on equal par,
If your knowledge to you is worth gaining
Then you'd better start fighting or you'll end up being sold,
For the times we must be a-changing.

Let's study inflation, pollution and war
And how the class structure makes people poor,
The causes of hatred, starvation and more;
For it's a new world we are creating;
We reject your illusions supporting these crimes,
For the times we must be a-changing.

12
Whither political economy?

At the start of 2009, the Department of Political Economy completed its first year in the new School of Social and Political Sciences in the Faculty of Arts. There were then six full-time ongoing academic staff positions—filled by Dick Bryan, Damien Cahill, Bill Dunn, Joseph Halevi, Stuart Rosewarne and Frank Stilwell—and two academic staff with fractional appointments—Tim Anderson and Elisabeth Riedl (the latter replacing Liz Hill for the second of her two years on leave in India). Joy Paton had been hired as an associate lecturer in 2008 to help ease the stresses of teaching that resulted from the surge of student enrolments that year: she was appointed to a lectureship for a further year in 2009. The growth of enrolments also led to the creation of new ongoing positions—with Susan Schroeder and Martijn Konings joining as lecturers in the second semester of 2009. Gavan Butler and Evan Jones continued as honorary associates, as did Ariel Saleh and Patricia Ranald who was appointed as an honorary associate in 2009.

The political economy staff are fewer in number than the mainstream economists—less than a third—but they constitute a coherent group in spite of their periodic personal and strategic differences. Additional tutors continue to be hired on a casual basis, as has become the norm in Australian universities, and they add significantly to the teaching capacity and vitality of the Department. Student enrolments have been growing substantially. The majority of those who take introductory units in political economy choose to go on to second and third-year studies in the subject and do so in a variety of degrees. Smaller numbers take the honours program in political economy, but those who have done so are some of the most capable people who have completed university courses in the social sciences. About twenty students were taking postgraduate research degrees in political economy in 2008. A new Master of Political Economy degree was approved in 2008 and took in its first students in 2009, immediately attracting strong enrolments.

Was the struggle to get to this point worthwhile? It certainly consumed much personal energy, as earlier chapters have illustrated. Yet without that struggle there would not be a Department of Political Economy in any Australian university. Islands of heterodoxy exist in departments of economics in a few other universities, but there is no other department that both protects and extends the traditions of political economy and assays the articulation of interdisciplinary connections with other social sciences. The University of Adelaide looked as though it might do at least the first in the 1970s under the leadership of Geoff Harcourt, but he left for Cambridge and the effort collapsed in the face of uncompromising neoclassicists. The strategy in some other universities of establishing one or more electives in heterodoxy and then seeking to build on these to create a major in political economy alongside studies in mainstream economics has not worked. There has been the odd success in instituting courses in social economics within mainstream departments—that is, the use of economic concepts in considering social policy questions—but, although that is to be applauded, it does not directly confront the hegemony of neoclassical economics.

The advocates of political economy at the University of Sydney believed that, after the early 1970s, they did not have much choice. There was no compromise offered. And, even if chipping away at the neoclassical structure from within the Department of Economics had had any prospect of opening up the study of political economy, there were hundreds of energetic students who would have had little truck with that incremental process. Clashing with the neoclassical structure and its defenders was compelling, heady stuff. Moreover, it had strong parallels with what colleagues were trying to do simultaneously in a few notable universities abroad.

Perhaps the political economists on the academic staff could have been kinder to their colleagues, less brash and more couth. To interject a personal note, we are sorry now that we did not handle ourselves better on some occasions. We must also concede that we did not succeed in changing mainstream economics; but nor has mainstream economics, as it has evolved, maintained a universally well-respected place in the new order. Economics generally is marginal within the new business and management schools and the forces that have created those new schools are, for the time being, stronger than the social science battalions can cope with.

Figure 45. Political economy students in the mid-1970s rally behind the demand for a separate department, which was eventually established in 2008.

What are the longer-term prospects? As ever, the broader national and international political economic environment influences the extent of interest in political economic alternatives. The prospects for teaching and research in political economy in the academy are not independent of the economic and political situation 'out there'. The so-called triumph of capitalism and the hegemony of neoliberal ideas and policy practices in the last two decades of the twentieth century were not conducive to the expansion and influence of critical political economy, other than as critique.

However, capitalism itself is fraught with contradictions and periodically teeters on the brink of crises. The first decade of the twenty-first century has seen major waves of corporate and financial collapses, social tensions arising from increasing economic inequalities, war, terrorism and dangerous environmental stresses. The problems of 'extreme' capitalism were starting to be acknowledged by even conservative politicians during 2008. It is increasingly recognised that the current capitalist system is neither economically stable nor ecologically sustainable.

By 2009 these tensions had become dramatic and the relevance of political economy had become urgently compelling. The new Obama Administration in Washington demanded that Congress approve its attempt to rescue the US economy from an ever-worsening crisis and proposed measures that are anathema to neo-liberals and neo-conservatives. The Administration spoke in terms that were unthinkable in Washington two years previously. Australia's prime minister published an essay that championed social democracy, a rebuilding of state regulation of financial systems and the development of new investment regimes. Generally it became clear again that 'the rule of the market' is a fiction and that all of the negotiations which underpin the behaviour of a capitalist economy have to be collectively monitored and governed. This has long been a major argument within the curriculum of political economy at the University of Sydney. The same position has characterised the articulation of political economy elsewhere, of course.

International movements promoting political economy in recent times have included the 'post-autistic' economics movement, starting in France in 2000. This was a significant movement although, apart from a successful online journal,[51] it did not maintain the momentum it originally promised. Other international organisations have been formed to coordinate the challenges to orthodox economics on an international scale. These include the International Initiative for the Promotion of Political Economy (IIPPE), the International Confederation of Associations for Pluralism in Economics (ICAPE), the Association for Social Economics and the Association for Evolutionary Economics. A heterodox economics newsletter (in electronic form), emanating from the USA, was started by Fred Lee in 2004 and continues to be circulated worldwide.[52] Conferences in heterodox economics are also occurring regularly now, providing focal points for exchange of ideas between challengers to the economic orthodoxy; the first such conference in Australia was organised by Peter Kriesler in 2002 at UNSW and the conference has since become an annual event.

There are other signs of maturity and influence. A continuing parade of impressive political economic publications (many of them from respected mainstream publishers such as Oxford University Press, Cambridge University Press, Macmillan, Routledge, Edward Elgar and

---

[51] The website is www.paecon.net/PAEReview/ ; see also K. Rankin, 'Autistic Economics?' *Journal of Australian Political Economy*, no. 50, December 2002, pp. 10–13; and E. Fullbrook (ed), *The crisis in economics: the post-autistic economics movement: the first 600 days*, Routledge, London, 2003.

[52] The website is www.heterodoxnews.com

Allen & Unwin) presents challenges to the prevailing economic orthodoxy. In 2005, UNSW introduced a political economy program in its School of Social Sciences and International Studies; units of study oriented towards political economy have also been developed at the University of Western Sydney and the University of Newcastle. In 2007, UNSW, in conjunction with the Centre for Full Employment at the University of Newcastle, also hosted the first conference/workshop for postgraduate research students studying heterodox economics and political economy at the various universities in the Sydney–Newcastle–Wollongong region.

The impediments to further progress and influence remain substantial. Opposition to political economy from the mainstream economists is still evident. As this book has shown, the roots of the mainstream are in a particular conceptual approach within the academic economics profession, one that effectively defines the economics discipline as being synonymous with that particular analytical vision known as neoclassicism. That has not fundamentally changed, although variations on the orthodoxy, such as game theory and behavioural economics, have been accommodated. Meanwhile, the desire of individuals to acquire power, and then to abuse that power once in high office is a perennial curse on the efficient and humane operation of social organisations. The behaviour of the academic elite in economics is an extreme case of this tendency, one that can best be likened to a jealous priesthood attempting the dogmatic imposition of a (secular) theology on succeeding generations of novices, and engaging in a persistent inquisition of heretics whenever such dissidence gains sufficient prominence to threaten entrenched holy writ.

The standard syllabus based on mainstream microeconomics and macroeconomic theory continues to be defended by its academic proponents on various grounds, the essences of which are captured by comments such as 'This is the body of analysis that we studied', 'This is what economics is', 'Students have to study it regardless of the lack of interest it engenders and regardless of its relevance' and 'Students have to be able to talk the language of the profession'. In this context, the best that one can hope for is a critical evaluation of orthodoxy, but on its own terms. Methodologically, this is a poor basis for the development of any critical perspective. Pedagogically, it is unsatisfactory because students complete their formal education with the suspicion that much of what they know is not to the point, but with exposure to only fragments of any alternative perspective.

The most plausible explanation for the ongoing dominance of the neoclassical perspective in the economics profession at large is a sociological one. New generations of adherents to intellectual orthodoxy are reproduced by a socialisation process enforced by lines of authority. The apparent cohesion of most economics departments elsewhere is not a product of open compromise between a variety of intellectual perspectives but the product of introverted narrowness.[53] These are exclusionary processes, a consequence of which is that individuals who have mastered the discipline's own apprenticeship are not readily permitted to follow a line of reasoning to whatever it leads. By analogy, those in authority stand firmly on the side of the church and against Galileo.

The entrenchment of orthodoxy in academic economics is paralleled in economic policy circles. Every country has its distinct policy

---

[53] An economics professor in another university in the Sydney metropolitan area in the 1970s was heard to remark on his concern to prevent an alternative political economy, University of Sydney style, from 'contaminating' his own department. Personal correspondence from a graduate (whose research work had been published in the *Journal of Australian Political Economy*) to one of the current authors in the 1990s tells of him being denied a tutorship in economics at another university because of his origins in the Sydney political economy program.

culture, and Australia in recent decades has had one of the most 'purist' economic policy cultures of any capitalist country. The reasons for this phenomenon are obscure, but part of the explanation surely lies in the monopolisation of official economic advice by the federal treasury (and its state and territory counterparts). The federal treasury houses the Productivity Commission, the official economic think tank through which all major government policy initiatives and program areas in crisis are passed for expert commentary. The Commission, which began life in 1974 as the Industries Assistance Commission, looks at these issues through a distinctively neoclassical economic lens. The agricultural economics fraternity, sizeable because of the economy's traditional dependence on agricultural exports, is similarly 'purist'; and yet the rural economy over which it presides is characterised by a uniqueness and complexity significantly divergent from the evident thinking of the agricultural economists. Well-endowed, corporate-funded think tanks reinforce the official line.[54]

The economic rationalists in the bureaucracy privilege simplistic (neoclassical) first principles over experience. Sources of evidence and opinion are narrowly circumscribed to like-minded organisations (with a preference for Anglo–America and its captive international organisations). Lateral thinking is eschewed. A striking example was provided by Treasury Secretary Ken Henry in a speech to Productivity Commission staff on 4 March 2008, titled 'Realising the vision'.[55] Henry applied *a priori* reasoning to opine that the free market mechanism was there to satisfy all needs and solve all problems,

---

[54] For fuller discussion of the biases in economic policy-making see E. Jones, 'The ascendancy of an idealist economics in Australia,' *Journal of Australian Political Economy*, no. 56, December 2002, pp. 44–71.

[55] K. Henry, 'Irrational fears of big bad markets hobble economy,' *The Australian*, 5 March, 2008.

individual and collective. Any adverse fallout could be readily dealt with through compensation under the generic welfare safety net (a net whose funding is perennially under attack from his own department). Henry's speech was mainly about the water crisis in Australia, and how application of conventional market principles would resolve the crisis. There was no acknowledgement of the unique and complex character of water availability and its supply, distribution and usage. He did not question whether God can be induced to generate higher rainfall with the promise of greater pecuniary rewards.

The edifice of economic policy advice has intermittently been challenged and modified, including by the efforts of political economy graduates after they joined the public service. The more pervasive feature, however, is the reproduction of the priestly mentality in the policy apparatus by new generations of graduates, often by US-trained economists, schooled in the entrenched academic orthodoxy. Reproduction is also facilitated by bipartisan political acceptance of the intellectual *status quo* (except for some parliamentarians from the National Party, the other minor parties or independents, who are then denigrated as troglodytes). The *status quo* has been reinforced by the effects of an independently generated managerialist revolution in public administration that has dictated a ruthless rules-bound process and by a hierarchy intolerant of alternative opinion. The dominant political class acquiesces, either through ignorance or cowardice, the latter fuelled by an aggressive finance sector and associated media.

In these circumstances, a political economy message faces powerful and intransigent forces, but at least political economy is well equipped to provide an analysis, an explanation of those forces and a language for those inclined to resist them. Although political economy has had little influence in most university economics departments, it has more traction in other academic disciplines. Indeed, the political economists at the University of Sydney have found encouragement from academics in such fields as geography, sociology, anthropology, political science, public health, and peace and conflict studies. Presumably, this encouragement partially reflects the shared wishes for exchanges of ideas rather than for the usual pontificating of mainstream economists.

Beyond the academy, the political economists have also developed good links with trade unions, social welfare organisations and a range of non-governmental organisations concerned with developing different 'voices' on political economic issues—such as the Australia Institute, Economic Reform Australia, the SEARCH Foundation, AFTINET, AidWatch, the Evatt Foundation, Catalyst and the Centre for Policy Development.

The final factor bearing on future prospects concerns government policies towards education. Here the situation is significantly different from what it was in the 1970s, when the struggle for university education in political economy began. Over the last two decades, the relentless squeeze on federal government funding of tertiary education has seen universities scrambling for alternative revenue sources, such as fee-paying students and corporate sponsorship. The universities have themselves adopted more corporate managerial models, thereby undermining the collegial structures that formerly existed.

Tertiary education has been restructured as, in effect, an industry: nowadays it often seems that the financial bottom line and position in published university 'league tables' are the most important concerns. From this perspective, the crucial survival test is the capacity to generate income over and above the niggardly public funding available for teaching non-fee-paying local students. The long-term consolidation and expansion of studies in political economy faces different challenges in this sort of educational environment.

How will this affect the students themselves? Will they continue in large numbers to be enthusiastic about studying political economy instead of (or sometimes in addition to) mainstream economics? Will their concern about major practical real world problems—poverty amid affluence, uneven development, climate change, financial crises and unemployment, terrorism and war—stimulate ongoing interest in probing the political economic causes, consequences and possible solutions? Is a political economic orientation with a focus on the 'big picture' compatible with an instrumental view of tertiary education as a means to a careerist end? Will the economic stresses on students, now causing most of them to be working many hours a week in paid jobs at the same time as they conduct their university studies, make them less involved in campus struggles such as those that led to the development of the political economy courses?

Our crystal ball clouds over at this point but, if the past is any guide to the future, one lesson from the political economy struggle is clear: cooperative and sustained commitment by students and staff is an essential ingredient for turning concern into challenge and struggle into success.

So, once more with feeling ...

> What do we want?
> Political economy.
> When do we want it?
> NOW!

The Economics Disaster

By PETER VAUGHAN

honi News Editor Peter Vaughan, outlines the present fiasco in the Faculty of Economics

Professor Hogan

Professor Simkin

Society elections. Peter Wright ran for the Presidency on the platform of supporting Waters in his attempts to reform the rapidly disintegrating economics courses. When the Economics Society found itself with a record turn-out for the election at 5 p.m. one Thursday afternoon, Wright's opponents, who included S.R.C. Rep. McKean, decided to jump on the bandwagon by adopting Wright's platform. Wright won the Presidency by a landslide of votes from enthusiastic Economics 1 and 2 students. Following Wright's success and popular pressure the Executive of department, if the growing discontent of the past months is any indication. It is unlikely that students can still be convinced of the necessity of including compulsory mathematical economics in its present form and degree of detail in the course. To delete mathematical economics from the course entirely would be completely out of keeping with international developments in the field. Rather the issue is the extent and relevance for pass students of mathematics in the present courses. To alter matriculation requirements in accord with the mathematical that they make allowance for students who do not aim for a career involving extensive mathematical analysis. Students not inclined in such a direction would be able to find some relevance in studying economics. Such courses would provide for the training of professional economists just as much as do Prof. Hogan's but not at the cost of all other students.

AGITATORS AND REPRISALS

However, reasonable requests and rational arguments do not of themselves guarantee success — even in an academic context. When Peter Wright presented the students' case at the Economics Faculty meeting last week Prof. Simkin attacked the Economics Society President, describing him as "mendacious". The Faculty Dean and Chairman of the meeting, Prof. Butlin, forced Simkin to retract the allegation that Wright was a liar. Simkin's reply to the students' suggested reforms involved references to "Victoria Lee-type agitators," the actual causes of discontent apparently escaping him. The issue will be discussed again when the Faculty hears a reply to the students' case from Profs. Hogan and Simkin and when, considers a motion to establish a staff-student departmental committee to handle such problems.

Meanwhile discontent grows. The weekly maths lectures in Economics 1 and 2 are now poorly attended and sometimes

Figure 46. Article in *Honi Soit* (extract, 18 June 1970) on the 'fiasco' that had developed in the Department of Economics (before the authors of this book began teaching there).

Chronology of principal events

1967

- Bruce Williams, a former economics professor, appointed Vice-Chancellor at the University of Sydney

1968

- Warren Hogan appointed as professor of economics

1969

- Colin Simkin appointed as second professor of economics
- Hogan and Simkin transform the syllabus in the Department of Economics, prioritising mainstream micro and macro theory and quantitative methods
- Tutors David Hill and Bill Waters help to conduct survey of students that reveals widespread dissatisfaction with the undergraduate economics curriculum and its teaching

1970

- Some academic staff in the Department of Economics call for independent inquiry into the department; Ted Wheelwright asks the Vice-Chancellor to initiate an inquiry by the University of Sydney Senate
- Employment of tutors Hill and Waters terminated by Professors Hogan and Simkin at the end of the year

1971

- Meetings held on campus to protest the sacking of Hill and Waters
- Waters elected as student representative on the Senate
- Dissident staff in the Department of Economics write memorandum setting out the case for considering radical critiques of mainstream economics throughout the department's curriculum

1972

- Geelum Simpson-Lee, Senior Lecturer in the Department of Economics, elected dean of the Faculty of Economics, a position he holds until 1978

1973

- Students organise conference on radical economics
- Strike in the Department of Philosophy over opposition to the introduction of a feminist course supported by many students in the Department of Economics
- Day of Protest organised by students in the Department of Economics as the culmination of several years of student discontent; normal lectures boycotted and alternative workshops held
- Proposals for an alternative undergraduate economics course developed by dissident students and staff
- Committee of inquiry into the Department of Economics established by the Faculty of Economics, and chaired by Pat Mills, Reader in Commercial Law

1974

- Mills committee report recommends creation of separate Department of Political Economy and full four-year program of political economy courses; a majority vote by the Faculty of Economics accepts the proposals
- Political Economy of Women elective introduced
- Dissident students in the Department of Economics organise Day of Outrage on the anniversary of the previous year's Day of Protest; lectures boycotted and alternative workshops held
- Proposal for the curriculum and teaching of new Economics I(P) and II(P) courses—the P standing for political economy—put to the Faculty of Economics
- University's Professorial Board approves the new courses
- Vice-Chancellor declines to create the new department recommended by the Faculty of Economics
- Petition by staff in the Department of Economics, calling for an elected departmental head, is ignored
- Employment of tutor Paul Roberts terminated by Professors Hogan and Simkin; tutor Jock Collins given a year's notice

1975

- Demonstrations held to protest victimisation of Roberts and Collins
- Economics I(P) introduced: taught by dissident Political Economy Group, comprising Ted Wheelwright, Geelum Simpson-Lee, Margaret Power, Gavan Butler, Frank Stilwell, Evan Jones, Debesh Bhattacharya, Louis Haddad and tutor Jock Collins

- Student Michael Brezniak suspended for leading a demonstration that disrupts a lecture by a visiting US academic addressing Professor Hogan's class; other students sign statutory declarations to say that they too disrupted the lecture

- Vice-Chancellor Bruce Williams addresses public meeting about the PE dispute; followed by students' demonstration at his office

- Ted Wheelwright rejected for third chair of economics and Gordon Mills is appointed instead; forty members of parliament call for an investigation; protests held on campus include noisy demonstration at the Senate meeting where the appointment is confirmed

- Professor Joan Robinson presents public lecture on the political economic challenge to mainstream economics

- Delay in approving Economics III(P) proposals leads to further protest activities; Vice-Chancellor's office occupied while he is at a Reserve Bank board meeting; Vice-Chancellor calls the police to evict the protesters

- Academic Board sets up committee of inquiry into political economy dispute; chaired by John Ward, professor of history

- Dissident staff give papers at national conference of economists in Brisbane, explaining their criticisms of mainstream economics (Stilwell and Butler on teaching of political economy; Jones on methodology)

- Political economy student Rod O'Donnell elected to University Senate and Academic Board for 1976; David Patch, also supporting political economy, elected as SRC President for 1976

1976

- Economics II(P) course begins
- Ward committee report recommends separate (temporary) unit of political economy; Academic Board accepts Ward report but Vice-Chancellor Williams rejects its principal recommendation
- Big demonstrations follow Vice-Chancellor's rejection of Ward committee proposal
- In July a Front-Lawn meeting is followed by forced entry and student occupation of the University administration building: Williams suspends three students
- University-wide strike by about 4000 students and staff in support of political economy, 14–26 July
- First national political economy conference (the first of seven annual conferences) held at the University of Sydney; attended by about 1500 people
- Rod O'Donnell re-elected to University Senate and Academic Board for 1977

1977

- First issue of *Journal of Australian Political Economy* published
- Students present petition to the professors of economics, setting out continuing grievances and demands for further reform

1978

- Political economy students, in conjunction with the SRC, organise a week of alternative educational events with the theme 'PE: still going strong'

- Prizes for top students in political economy established, named in honour of famous political economists: John Kenneth Galbraith, Joan Robinson, Paul Sweezy and Gunnar Myrdal

1979

- Fourth national PE conference held at University of Sydney

1980

- Stephen Salsbury, an opponent of the political economy activists, becomes dean of the Faculty of Economics, a position he holds until 1988, and then 1991–1999

1981

- Historian John Ward becomes Vice-Chancellor after retirement of Bruce Williams
- Political economy students and staff demand allocation of more resources to political economy program and introduction of third-year and honours courses in political economy; petition signed by 700 students handed to Vice-Chancellor; demonstration at Vice-Chancellor's office
- Statement about inadequate provision of senior courses and inadequate staffing signed by seven PE staff and published in *Honi Soit*
- Vice-Chancellor Ward asks the Academic Board to set up new committee of inquiry into the Department of Economics; committee chaired by G.A. Wilkes, professor of English literature

1982

- Wilkes committee report recommends that new third and fourth-year courses in political economy be introduced; emphasises need for freedom of movement for students and transfer of teaching expertise; recommends that one of the political economists be given the status of 'professor most concerned'; gives tentative support for additional degree in Economic and Social Sciences

- Political economists support Wilkes proposals, albeit with reservations, and present proposals for course changes consistent with those guidelines: the mainstream economists develop different proposals that would eradicate Economics I(P) and II(P) in favour of common courses

- Fearing the loss of distinct 'P' courses, PE student activists set up protest tent in the Quad and stay overnight

- Seventh national PE conference held at University of Sydney

1983

- Academic Board recommends that Department of Economics reconsider its course structure, that political economy be formally recognised as a full three-year and honours program, but that no separate Department of Political Economy be created

- The professors of economics, supported by the Vice-Chancellor, propose to do away with Economics I(P) and II(P), under the guise of course restructuring

- These proposals lead to demonstrations at Vice-Chancellor's office and at Professorial Board meeting

- SRC referendum of students (including mainstream economics students) supports retention of separate mainstream economics and political economy courses
- Political economy students park a caravan on the Front Lawn for three weeks as focal point for protest
- Special issue of *Honi Soit* published on the continuing PE dispute
- Front-Lawn rally on 15 June, followed by occupation of clock tower at the Quad
- Merewether Building occupied by student protesters on 29 June; New South Wales Police Tactical Response Group brought in to end the demonstration; students leave but reoccupy the building on 5 July and continue the occupation for another nine days
- Five students suspended by the Vice-Chancellor for their part on the demonstrations; four more also required to face charges before the Proctorial Board
- Vice-Chancellor Ward agrees to create the position of director of 'P' courses in the Department of Economics (a position occupied for the next ten years by Associate Professor Stilwell)
- Penalties imposed by the Proctorial Board on the nine students facing disciplinary proceedings range from a reprimand to a $100 fine plus a 'suspended suspension' (i.e. suspension from classes not imposed unless the student is guilty of further misconduct)

1984

- Combined first-year economics course introduced (with political economy teachers responsible for teaching the second of the three terms)
- Vice-Chancellor proposes shifting some parts of the Faculty of Economics, including the Department of Government as well as political economy, to a new faculty, generating a university-wide debate on the pros and cons of various alternative arrangements: nothing results

1985

- Stephen Salsbury, dean of the Faculty of Economics, sets up committees to create two different degrees, one requiring mainstream economics and the other permitting the study of political economy and social sciences; proposals approved by the Faculty of Economics, the Academic Board and subsequently by the Senate

1986

- Retirement event for Ted Wheelwright attracts more than 300 people; speeches by Bob Debus, Hugh Stretton and Alan Ashbolt
- First cohort of students to graduate with study of political economy in their BEc honours degree: Anne Franco, Terry Flew, Simon Draper, Peter Colley and George Argyrous

1987

- Two new degrees begin: a revised BEc, with three years compulsory mainstream economics, and new BEc(SocSc), which offers students a choice of either mainstream economics or political economy

- Economics I(P)—now called Economics I(SocSc)—is restored
- Political economist J.K. Galbraith presents a public lecture at the University at the start of the new BEc(SocSc) degree

1990

- First political economy honours students graduate from BEc(SocSc) degree
- MEc(SocSc) degree with honours is introduced, allowing students to study political economy at postgraduate level

1994

- Conference held at University of Sydney to celebrate twenty years of Political economy courses and twenty-one years of the Political Economy of Women

1997

- First student to graduate with PhD from the Discipline of Political Economy: Bill Lucarelli
- New MEc(SocSc) in Australian Political Economy introduced

1998

- Staff teaching the political economy courses move temporarily (for two years) from the Merewether Building into the Press Building

1999

- Peter Wolnizer appointed as dean of the Faculty of Economics
- BEc(SocSc) degree restructured as Bachelor of Economic and Social Sciences

2000

- Faculty of Economics becomes Faculty of Economics and Business; newly created School of Economics and Political Science and School of Business replace the former departments. The Discipline of Political Economy is established within the former school, separate from the Discipline of Economics. Its permanent staff at this time comprises two associate professors (Dick Bryan and Frank Stilwell), four senior lecturers (Gavan Butler, Evan Jones, Joseph Halevi and Stuart Rosewarne), two lecturers (Pamela Cawthorne and Gabrielle Meagher) and two half-time associate lecturers (Elizabeth Hill and Shaun Wilson)

2001

- Frank Stilwell appointed to a personal professorship, making him the first professor of political economy

2002

- *Journal of Australian Political Economy* publishes its fiftieth issue, with a special theme 'The state of political economy'
- Faculty of Economics and Business closes the Discipline of Economic History

2003

- Conference held at the University of Sydney to consider new directions for education in political economy

2004

- Political economy staff who retire this year and next—Dr Gavan Butler, Dr Pamela Cawthorne and Associate Professor Evan Jones—are not replaced

- Social event held to celebrate thirty years of political economy courses at the University of Sydney

2006

- PE staff become increasingly fearful of prospects of the discipline's survival in the Faculty of Economics and Business
- PE student activists picket Faculty of Economics meeting, demanding guarantee for the long term future of the PE discipline, lifting the PE staffing freeze and an end to financial discrimination against courses that have a high proportion of HECS students
- Political Economy Alumni Association holds its first meeting, chaired by Eleanor Hall from the ABC and addressed by Greg Combet, ACTU national secretary (both former PE students)
- Provost establishes committee of inquiry into the future of the social sciences, chaired by Professor Tom Kvan, dean of the Faculty of Architecture; report recommends that the Discipline of Political Economy (and the Discipline of Government and International Relations) be repositioned in new School of Social Inquiry in the Faculty of Arts

2007

- Provost accepts Kvan committee's recommendations and establishes committee to implement them, chaired by Stephen Garton, dean of the Faculty of Arts
- Dean of Arts establishes committees to amalgamate undergraduate degrees: Bachelor of Economic and Social Sciences and Bachelor of International Studies to be combined with existing Arts degrees; other degrees in which political economy can be studied continue unchanged

2008

- Political economy begins new era as separate department within the School of Social and Political Sciences in the Faculty of Arts
- Student enrolments surge, with 600 starting the introductory unit of study 'Economics as a Social Science' and over 750 in the two first year units in second semester
- Annual E.L. 'Ted' Wheelwright Memorial Lecture introduced; inaugural lecture given by Professor Walden Bello from University of the Philippines
- Dick Bryan promoted to professorship in political economy

2009

- New degree of Master of Political Economy introduced, replacing the previous MEc(SocSc), and immediately attracts good enrolments
- Academic Board approves new degree of Bachelor of Political Economic and Social Sciences, replacing the Bachelor of Economic and Social Sciences degree. Political economy is one of the core subjects for the degree, which begins in 2010
- Faculty of Arts review of the Department of Political Economy, conducted by external assessors, reports favourably on the department and emphasises that it can strengthen its profile as a nationally and internationally recognised centre for teaching and research.

Figure 47. 2008 poster.

Index

Entries in **BOLD** indicate posters and photographs

Abbott, Tony 47, 80, **81**
academic authority xii
  see also power
Academic Board 40, 42, 58–9,
  61, 63–70, 128, 137, 161, 165
  Faculty of Social Sciences
  proposal 70
academic conflict vii
Academics' Union 159
  see also National Tertiary
  Education Union; Sydney
  Association of University
  Teachers
accounting ix, 86, 91
Ackerman, F. 109
AFTINET 190
agricultural economics 188
AidWatch 190
Aints, The 132
Albanese, Anthony 63
Alexander, Hal 51
Althusser, Louis 179
Altman, Dennis 160
Anderson, Tim 84, 165, 175

Argyrous, George 88–9, 170
Armstrong, David 162, 163
Australian Association for
  Cultural Freedom 1
Australian Labor Party (ALP) 1,
  37, 88
Australian Political Economy
  Movement (APEM) 167, 169
Austrian school 110

Bachelor of Commerce courses
  83
Bachelor of Economics (Social
  Sciences) 78–87, 152, 171
Bachelor of International
  Studies 91
Baird, Marion 115–16
Baker, Lance 46
Barac, Maria 61, 65, **66, 155**
behavioural economics 108, 185
Bello, Walden 206
Bhattycharya, Debesh x, 5, 31,
  84, 115
Black, Hermann 4
Bowles, Sam xiii, 56

Brennan, Theresa 179
Brezniak, Michael 11, 13, 28–9, 33, **45**, 53, 56, 57, 143, 145–7
Brown, Gavin 96
Browning, R. 150
Bryan, Dick xix, 84, 98, 165, 167, 170, 174, 175
Buchanan, James 110
Buckley, Ken 14, 28–9, 51, 53, 143, 146, 170
Bulletin, The 80, **81**, 150
Burgess, John xviii–xix
Burnheim, John 162, 163, 164
Burrell, Steve 33, 36
Burton, Steve 57
Business Studies courses and economics 82–4, 87, 120, 183
Butcher, Ben Spies 100
Butler, Gavan x, 5, 7, 19, 115, 127, **130**, 175, 181
   Academic Board 166
   common course teaching 138
   debate 1974 17
   Faculty meetings 50
   newspaper article 96
   retirement 92
   Roberts sacking document 28

Cahill, Damien 167
Callus, Ron 79
Campbell, Keith 162
Carson, Rachel 165
Catalyst 190

Cawthorne, Pamela 92, 165
Centre of Full Employment and Equity (CofFEE) 186
Centre for Independent Studies (CIS) 149
Centre for Policy Development 190
Centre for Social Leadership 71
Chaples, Ernie 160
Chicago School 110
Clark, David xiv, 32, 80, 153, 172
classical political economy x, xi
Clock Tower occupation 61, **62**
Club of Rome 165
Coase, Ronald 110
Cohen, Dinah 33
Collins, Ian 33
Collins, Jock 27–8, 32, 50–3, 56, 143, 179
Combet, Greg 100, 157
commerce versus economics 83
Communist Club 47
community and labour movement 2
competition 105–6
   see also markets; neoclassical economics
Connell, R.W. xii, 160
Conrade, Marijke 65
cops on campus 36, 65, **72**
corporate sponsorship 148–9

Council for Academic Freedom
and Democracy in Australia
(CAFDA) 32
Cozijn, John 167
Crittenden, P. 163
Crough, Greg 8, 55
Curthoys, Jean 162, 163, 164

degree restructures 97
see also business studies;
faculty structures
Democratic Labor Party (DLP)
47
Department of Economic
History 126, 161
Department of Economics ix
Academic Board demands
1983 63–5
business degrees and 87–8,
90–1, 183
common course design 68–9
curriculum restrictions 3–4
Hogan proposal for common
course 59
1971 mid-year staff meetings
7–8
power within 27–8, 122, 134,
172, 182–3
student delegation to, 1981 57
teaching standards 4–5, 14,
119–21, 177
Wilkes report 59
Williams refusal of PE courses
and 25, 34–5

Department of Government and
Public Administration ix, xii,
70, 93, 126
Department of Industrial
Relations 126, 160
Department of Philosophy
dispute 9, 19, 162
Department of Political
Economy
Academic Board and 70
enrolments 176–7
Mills report recommendation
for 14, 36
Department of Social Work 160
Department of Sociology 161
Department of Work and
Organisational Studies 115,
130
Devitt, Michael 162
Discipline of Government and
International Relations 93,
95–6
Discipline of International
Business 92
Discipline of Political Economy
87, 91, 128
finances of the Faculty and
92–3, 151
range of views viii–ix, 11,
175–6
resource squeeze 91–2, 151
disciplines xv, 91
discrimination against PE
courses 142–3

Dunn, Bill 91, 170

economic history x, 110
economic journalism xiv
economic policy, keeping PE
  views out 188
Economic Record 173
Economic Reform Australia
  190
economics
  alternative teaching proposal
    19, 21–2
  commercialism and xv, 83
  market behaviour as focus ix
  mathematical focus 4–5, 20
  narrowing approaches 4
  versus commerce 83
  what's wrong with its teaching
    104–15
  see also neoclassical
    economics
Economics I and Economics II
  (1969) 6–7
Economics I(P) 19, 31, 57–8,
  63–4, 165
Economics II(P) 22, 31, 33, 56,
  57–8, 63–4
Economics Society of Australia
  and New Zealand 32, 173
ECOPSoc 94, 100, 101–3, 154,
  157, **206**
Edsall, Sally 33, 131–3
Ellis, Jude 33

employment prospects 29, 30,
  32, 80–3, 121–2, 153
  political economy as a
    strength xv–xvi, 154–5
environmentalism 165
equilibrium theory 105–6
Evatt Foundation 190

Faculty of Arts xv, 95–9, 161
  fit of political economy with
    99–101, 128, 176
  increasing research strengths
    of 98
  philosophy dispute in 162–3
Faculty of Economics xv, 13
Faculty of Economics and
  Business 91–2, 98–9, 183
  finances within 92–4, 121–2,
    151–2
  Board 50–1
  fee income dependence 150–
    3, 190
  inquiry into economics
    teaching 14
  promotions committee and
    PE staff 32, 41, 56, 139–40
  recommendations of Mills
    report 17–18, 22, 36
  Salsbury and separate degree
    program 78
  support within for PE 161
  Wolnizer and 86–7

faculty structures,
  reorganisation of xv, 78–87, 95–9
fee paying students 93–4, 150–3, 190
feminism 3, 9, 19, 163, 164
Ferguson, Laurie **45**
Ferris, Peter 57
Fields, Richard 8, 9, 10, 18, 55
Flannery, Kristie 94
Fraser, Malcolm 49, 88
Free University xii
Freire, Paulo xiii
French Society 47
Friedman, Milton 108
Fullbrook, E. 109

Galbraith, J.K. 141, **171**
game theory 108–9, 185
Geitzelt, Arthur 37
gender 3, 164
General Agreement on Trade in Services (GATS) 132
Gintis, Herb xiii, 56
Gittins, Ross 155, 174
global financial crisis 122
Glyn, Andrew 172
Gough, Ian 56
Gration, Chris 63, 65, **155**
Green Bans 2
Groenewegen, Peter 17, 118, 124, 153
  BEc (Social Sciences) 79–80

  objections to PE courses 1974 22
  objections to PE honours 31–2
  Professorial appointment 141–2
  retired 90
  Wheelwright course proposal 137

Haddad, Louis x, 5, 31
Haddad, Maurice x, 5, 7
Halevi, Joseph 84, 170
Hamilton, Clive 33, 145–7, 170
Harcourt, Geoff 32, 49, 174, 182
Harding, Ann 55–6
Hargreaves Heap, Shaun 172
Hawke, Bob 88
Henry George League 18
Henry, Ken 188
Heterodox Economics 168, 185
Hill, David 6, 50, 131
Hill, Liz 84, 165
Himmelweit, Susan 172
Hirst, Martin 33, 36–8, **43**, 46, 51, 179
Hogan, Michael 79
Hogan, Warren ix, x, 50, 124, 140, **192**
  BEc (Social Sciences) 80, **81**, 154
  Centre for Independent Studies (CIS) 149

day of protest 1973 and 11–12
debate 1974 17
Department of Government and Public Admin and 136
Groenewegen professorship and 142
mathematical focus 3–4, 5
meeting with students 1981 57
Mills report and 17
objections to alternative courses 22, 33, 143, 145–7
Roberts dismissal 28
retired 90
student dissatisfaction with 6, 7, 19, 145–6
Wilkes report and 59
Hollis, M. 109
Honi Soit 6, 10, 28, 92–3, 94, **95, 177, 192**
Hood, Darryl 33
Howard government 90

Illich, Ivan xiii
individualism 104
institutionalism xi, 107, 113, 175
intellectual suppression 134–47
International and Global Studies 98
International Confederation of Associations for Pluralism in Economics (ICAPE) 185
International Initiative for the Promotion of Political Economy (IIPPE) 185
International Socialists 38, 180
international students 93–4, 150–3, 190
Irons, Stephen 14
Irving, Terry xii, 160
Itoh, Makato 172

Jacka, Liz 163, 164
Jackson, Michael 160–1
Jefferis, Chris 100
Jenkins, Rhys 172
Jones, Alex 163
Jones, Evan x, xix, 5, 31, 109, 114, 181
  common course teaching 69, 138
  Faculty meetings 50
  JAPE 53
  methodology 173
  PE staffing and tenure 32, 139, **177**
  resistance to course proposal of 136
Journal of Australian Political Economy xix, 52, 53, 143, 169, 187
journalism and political economy studies 154–5
Joyce, Michael 33

Kalecki, Michael 144

Keen, Steve 8, 9–10, 13, 18–20, 33, **45**, 55, 109, 170, 174
  Debunking Economics 174
Kerr, Sir John 49
Kerridge, Graham 14
Keynes, John Maynard 3, 20, 89, 107
Keynesianism 107–8, 113
Kiernan, Eric 79
King, Peter 160, 179
Kobetsky, Mike 33
Konings, Martijn 181
Kramer, Leonie 85, 166
Kriesler, Peter 185
Kuhn, Rick 33, 170, 178–80
Kuhn, Thomas 114
Kvan, Tom 96–7

Labor Club 47
labour markets 111
Laffer, Kingsley 160
Lanahan, Bruce 33, 179, 180
Lane-Mullins, Francis Xavier 48
Leigh, Michael 138, 160
Levien, Harold 52
Liberal Club 47
Liberal Party 149
Lucarelli, Bill 170
Luscombe, Daniel 63

McAndrew, Kevin 33
McCormack, Amanda 94, 101–3

McFarlane, Bruce 18
McGuinness, Padraic P. xiv, 29–30, 80, 153
macroeconomics 4–5, 107
Madge, Alan 33
Maiden, Valerie 33
mainstream economics
  failings of 20
  narrowness of 4, 5, 82, 173, 188–90
  see also economics; markets; neoclassical economics
Malthus, Thomas x
managerialism 189, 190
Marglin, S. 109
market behaviour, mainstream economics focus ix
markets
  perfect competition idea 104, 16–7, 122
  public policy and 188–90
  questioning of in broader society 184
  student numbers and staffing 148–55
Marx, Karl x
Marxism xi
Marxist economics x, 107, 113, 175
Master of Economics (Social Sciences) 84
Masters in Political Economy 93–4, 182
mathematics 3, 4–5,

failures of mainstream economics teaching shown by 20
Mathews, Trevor 179
Meagher, Gabrielle xix, 84, 165, 170, 174
Meaney, Neville 166
methodology 173, 187
Meyering, Isobelle Barrett 94, 95
microeconomics 4–5
Milgate, Murray 68
Mill, James x
Mill, John Stuart x
Mills, Gordon 56, 79, 90, 124
Mills, Pat 14
Mills report recommendations 14, 20, 36
Mohun, Simon 172
Molnar, George 162
monetarism 108
Mortimer, Rex 14
Moss, Scott 57
Movement for Political Economy 46
Movement of Active Socialists 38
Myrdal, Gunnar 172

Nadal, A. 109
Nanson, Angela 33, 51
National Centre for Social and Economic Modelling (NATSEM) 56
National Civic Council (NCC) 49
National Tertiary Education Union (NTEU) 167
National Times 29–30
Nell, Ed 49, 56, 109
neoclassical economics x, xi, 104–15, 146, 182, 187
  application to real world and employment 121–2
  variants to 108–10
new growth theory 108
new institutionalism 110
New Left 2–3
NSW Teachers' Federation 131–3
Nicol, Bill 19, 33
North, Douglass 110
Nutbeam, Don 96

O'Donnell, Carol 37
O'Donnell, Rod 29, 37, **39**, 44–5, 51, 56, 127, 170
O'Neil, Professor 50
O'Neill, Steve 57
O'Shaughnessy, Terry 57
Openshaw, Mark 33
Ormerod, P. 109
overseas fee paying students, language difficulties and 93

paradigm shifts 111, 114
Patch, David 37, 47
Paton, Joy 181

Patten, Paul 179
pedagogy xii, xiii, 184-8
  political economy approach
    and 113-14, 118-30, 184-8
perfect competition 105
  see also markets
Peterson, Kathi 33, **34**
Phillips, Chris 33
Phillips, Lorraine 33
Phipps, Tony 68
Pickette, Rod 33
political economy
  broad influence of this
    approach 183-8
  conference posters **53-5**(between)
  "Faculty" caravan **60**, 61-2, 72, **73,75**
  first National Conference 1976 49, 52,55
  great variety of viewpoints within viii-ix, 11, 175
  historical and empirical basis of 113-14
  international disputes in teaching xiii, 160
  legitimacy of 165-75
  National Conferences 1979 55, 168
  new building for the Group 85, **86**
  separate discipline established 87
  using the name at Sydney Uni 11
  versus mainstream economics viii
  Vice-Chancellor and new department 1974 22-4
  what is it? x-xi
  WHEN DO WE WANT IT? NOW! vii. 191
Political Economy Alumni Society 100, 101-3, 155, 156-8
political economy courses
  cartoon comment 77
  corporations and 148-50
  demand to extend 33-5, 57-9
  discrimination against 142-3
  disparagement of by journalists 29-30, 153-4
  employment prospects of students and 29, 30, 32, 80-3, 121-2, 153
  ending separate 1st year courses 63-4
  engagement with the struggle and friendship xiv, 132
  feminism and 164, 175
  interdisciplinary studies and 160-6
  international support for 160-1, 170-1
  settled state of from mid 1980s 76

staffing and 1974 and 1975 21–2, 31–2, 139
tenure 41, 139–40
3rd year courses 31–2, 33, 41, 56, 63
Wilkes and Hogan proposals 59–60
Political Economy Group 119, 183–4
new building for the Group 85, **86**
staffing and tenure 32, 57, 120–1, 139
student load 57, 65, 84–5, 181
Political Economy honours 31–2, 137–8, 143–4
Political Economy Hour 55
Political Economy song 180
political economy publications 170, 185–6
Political Economy Students Assn 55, 71
political economy students society 94, 100, 101–3, 154, 157, **206**
Politics in the Pub 168
Popper, Karl 114
Porteous, Paul 61, 65, 71–5
post–autistic economics 185
post–Keynesianism 113, 175
power
neoclassical economics and 112, 185

of teachers over students xii, 6, 13, 22, 94–5, 119, 122–30
pedagogy and 118–30
professorial 5, 6, 22, 27–8, 35, 40, 160
study of ix, xi, 122–3
suppression of PE and 134–47
Power, Margaret x, 5, 31, 50, 84, 164
Pritchard, Hugh x, 52
Productivity Commission 188
professorial appointments 32–3, 37, 51, 56, 140–1
Professorial Board 22, 25–6, 40, 56, 122
public choice theory 110
Pusey, M. 110

quarantining PE 187
radical economics course proposal 1973 8
Ranald, Pat 181
rational expectations theory 108
rationalism 104, 106, 110
Re, David 63
Rees, Stuart 160
Renwick, Cyril 107
reproduction of the social order 187
Ricardo, David x, xi
Riedl, Elisabeth 181
risk management 92

Roberts, Paul 27-9, 33
Robinson, Joan 33, 112, 141, 170-1
Rodrigo, Darren 100, 156-8
Rorris, Adam 63, **155**
Rosewarne, Stuart xix, 53, 84, 165, 167, 174, 175
Ross, Russell 68
Rowthorn, Bob 172

sackings of staff 6, 27
Saints, The 132
Saleh, Ariel 181
Salsbury, Stephen 76
 marginalising PE 77-8, 127, 130, 150, 154
 student occupation and 76-7
 unforeseen consequences of his approach 83-4
Samson, Anna 100
Samuelson, Paul 8-9, 10
Saunders, David 161
School of Business 87, 91
School of Economics and Political Science 87, 92
Schools of Social and Political Sciences xv, 97-101
Schroeder, Susan 181
Search Foundation 168, 190
Senate 127, **129**
Sharpe, Ian 22
Short, Kate 57
Sicklen, Derek 33

Simkin, Colin ix, x, 50, 114, 124, 140, **192**
 Centre for Independent Studies (CIS) 149
 graffiti damage 29, **48**
 mathematical focus 3-4, 5
 retirement 141
 Samuelson visit 8-9
 student dissatisfaction with 6, 7, 18
Simpson-Lee, Geelum x, 5, 31
 Dean 13-14, 51
 economics textbook 107
 prize in honour of 172
 promotions committee and PE staff 32, 56, 139, 140-1
 retirement 76
Sinclair, June 95
Skellern, Jeremy 94
Smith, Adam x
Smith, Bernard 161
Smith, Chris 33
Smith, Terry 161
social change and protest 1, 2
Socialist Alternative 38
Spice, Greg 57
Stephen Roberts Lecture Theatre 29
Stilwell, Frank x, xix, 115, **125, 130**
 Academic Board 166
 Associate Professorship 64
 broad recognition 174

common course design and teaching 68, 69, 138
debate 1974 17
Economics as a Social Science 170
Faculty meetings 50, 51
Faculty restructure and 98
Economics I teaching early 1970s 7–8, 18
environmental concerns 165
JAPE 53
lecturing quality 156
Political Economy: the contest of economic ideas 170
PE staffing and tenure 32, 64–5
range of viewpoints in PE 175
Readings in Political Economy 170
regional and urban economics course 136
Roberts sacking document 28
Salsbury proposals and 79
Simkin retirement and 141–2
Stokes, Nigel 6–7
Stove, David 162, 163
Stretton, Hugh 19–20
student activism
and political economy xiv, 36–7, 72–5, 132, 159, 183
clock tower 62
conservative opposition to 1, 159

day of outrage 1974 xv, **15**, 23, **24**
day of protest 1973 10
debate poster 1974 **16**, 17
early protest image **10**
Front Lawn rally 1975 **54, 125**
general strike 46, 52, 132, 163
international social protest 2
lobbying for resources 94
mass meeting with Vice-Chancellor **30**
Merewether building 65–7, 71, 76, 94
1969 economic restructure and dissatisfaction 6
petition for more PE 58
philosophy dispute and 9, 19, 162
professorial power fire! **35**, 160
protest 1975 **xvii**
protest posters 1974 **12, 26, 117, 123**
Quadrangle **xx, 63, 64**, 71, **133, 183**
radical political economics conference 1973 8, 18, **54**, 106
resolve or resign protests 46–7
Roberts dismissal 28

Vice-Chancellor's office
  occupation xv, 34-5, 38, **39**, 116
Ward Committee recommendations and 44
student evaluation methods 119
student fees 91, 151-3, 190
Student Representative Council (SRC) 47, 55, 59-60
students and careers
  political economy as a strength xv-xvi, 29, 30, 32, 80-3, 121-2, 153, 154-5
  friendships xix
Suchting, Wal 162
Sweezy, Paul 172
Sydney Association of University Teachers (SAUT) 141, 166
  see also Academics Union; National Tertiary Education Union (NTEU)
Sydney University Economics Society (SUES) 13, 132
Sydney University Press building 85, **86**
Symbionese Liberation Army 23

teaching, quality of 4-5, 6-7, 14, 19, 118 30, 173, 177
The Australia Institute 190
Thompson, Herb 174
Thornton, Kathy 33

Thurow, Lester 109
Times Higher Educational Supplement 98
Titterton, Louise 57
Tom Robinson Band 133
Toner, Phil 170
Toohey, Brian 105
trade unions 2, 112, 159, 166-7, 190
Transnational Corporations Research Centre 32, 149-50
Treasury 188

university fees 36, 190
university governance
  power structures 5, 6, 13, 22-3, 26-9, 122-30, 134, 142, 185-6
University of Adelaide 182
University of NSW political economy courses 186
University of Newcastle 186
University of Sydney ix
  commercial reorientation of studies xv, xix, 82-4, 86-7, 90-1, 151-3

Vice-Chancellor
  burning effigy of **35**
  demonstration 1981 58
  mass meeting **30**
  occupation of office 1975 xv, 34-5, 38, **39**

power of 22-5, 27, 122, **123**, 141-2
refuses a separate department 23, 25
Ward recommendations and 44
Vietnam War 1, 2, 36
Vineberg, Steve 33

Walters, Linda 33
Ward, B. 109
Ward Committee 40-1
Ward, John 32, **43**, 49, **66**
  common courses and 63-70
  PE staffing 64-5
  Vice-Chancellor 58, 127, 128
  see also Vice-Chancellor
Waters, Bill 6, 50, 106, 127
Watson, Lex 160
Wells, Murray 85, 171
Westmore, Tony 63
Westpac 149
Wheelwright, Ted x, 5, 7, 31, 88, 106, 114, 127, 132, 139, 149-50
  common course design 68, 69
  Essays in the Political Economy of Australian Capitalism 170
  Faculty meetings 50
  figurehead and publications 51-2, 170

Memorial Lecture series **206**
prize in honour of 172
quality of lecturing 51
Readings in Political Economy 170
refused vacant chair in economics 32-3, 37, 51, 140-1
retirement 84
3rd year course proposal and 137
Whitlam Government 36, 49
Wilkes committee 63-70
Wilkes, Gerry 58-9, 69
Williams, Bruce ix, 4, 23, 25, 34-5, 38, 128, **130, 147**, 179
  SAUT and 167
  Simkin retirement and 141-2
  sociology and 161-2
  student activism and 159-60
  Ward recommendations and 41, 44-8, 52
  see also Vice-Chancellor
Wilson, Jeffrey 94, 95
Wolnizer, Peter 86-7, 128, 150
Wran, Neville 6-7

Yates, Judy 68
Yen, Stephen 61, **75**

www.ingramcontent.com/pod-product-compliance
Lightning Source LLC
Chambersburg PA
CBHW071817230426
43670CB00013B/2481